UNDERSTAN[...]
PROPERTY I[...]

W.T. Murphy and Simon Roberts teach at the London School of Economics and Political Science.

J.A.G. Griffith is Emeritus Professor of Public Law in the University of London.

Understanding Law
Editor: J.A.G. Griffith

W.T. Murphy and
Simon Roberts

UNDERSTANDING
PROPERTY LAW

Fontana Press

First published in 1987 by Fontana Paperbacks
8 Grafton Street, London W1X 3LA

Set in 10 pt Times

Made and printed in Great Britain by
William Collins Sons & Co. Ltd, Glasgow

Contents

Contents

Contents

Editor's Preface

This series is directed primarily at two groups of readers: the general reader who wishes to understand what it is that lawyers are talking about and the law student who is told that he is about to study a subject called tort, or contract, or criminal law, or property, or trusts and equity, or public law. These titles convey little that is clear about the nature of their subjects and the extra-legal meanings that attach to some – such as contract or criminal law – may be misleading.

Each book in this series seeks to explain what the subject is about, what are the special kinds of problems it seeks to solve, and why it has developed as it has. The books are not at all meant to be summaries of their subjects, each of which covers a complicated area of human activity.

The law student will, in his or her course, be expected to read much longer and fuller texts on the subjects, to attend lectures and tutorials. The books in this series seek to provide introductions to be read early in the course or before it begins. It is hoped that these introductions will enable the student to grasp the essentials before coming to grips with the details. So also, the general reader who wishes to pursue the subject more fully will have to read the more detailed texts.

Although these books are intended to be introductions, they are not meant to be simplifications. These are not 'easy' books, however clearly they are written. Understanding law is not an easy matter. This is not, as is often said, primarily because lawyers use words with special meanings. It is because law has to deal with the complications, both personal and commercial, that people become involved in. We are all as busy as ants, more purposeful and sometimes less efficient. Law tries to regularise these complications and so cannot avoid being itself complicated.

The intention of the series will be achieved if the books give the reader a broad perspective and a general understanding of the legal principles on which these different subjects are based.

John Griffith
April 1987

Authors' Preface

There is no single way of introducing the study of the English law of property. The approach adopted here, for good or bad, is 'historical', in some sense. What follows is not, to be sure, a 'narrative', but a selective 'looking back' at aspects of the past which, in our view, shed light upon the present. Such an approach takes content, and the context of the content, seriously, if selectively, and places great stress on the concerns which underscored and motivated the generation of the materials which the student encounters. Of course an introduction of this kind involves the problem of presenting the subject in a way that led Milsom recently to observe that in parts of 'our books on property law . . . the reader can sometimes wonder what century he is in' (1981:viii). But that is the point. It is not clear what century we are in, because the mind of the English property lawyer inhabits many centuries as if they were all part of the present. This is not a criticism: lawyers have a job to do and that job is not to write more history books but to get on and deal with what presses in the present. So this is an auto-combustible text. It assumes that the student needs to know something of the past to get a grip on the present; but once that grip is reasonably secure, it assumes that he or she, in turning from contemplation (if student life can still be so described) to activity, to the work of the world, will forget these reminiscences in the course of getting on with the task to hand.

Much of this book owes its genesis to our experience of teaching property law to Intermediate students at the London School of Economics. Some of it derives from a handout for students prepared by the first-named author, who would also like to thank the participants in a research seminar at University College London for their comments on a paper dealing with 'English Formalism'.

Pages 171–3 largely reproduce a section of a paper prepared for the Istituto di Diritto Comparato in Florence, 'The Right to Housing and the English Legal Tradition'.

We have run up many debts in the preparation of the present work. In particular, we would like to thank (without associating them with its many flaws) Stuart Anderson, Joe Jacob, Martin Loughlin, Martin Partington, Alison Real and Colin Scott.

1

What Is Property?

. . . English legal thought is essentially an empirical art. . . . The
legal thinking of the layman is . . . literalistic. He tends to be a
definition-monger when he believes he is arguing 'legally'. Closely
connected with this trait is the tendency to draw conclusions from
individual case to individual case. . . . In both respects . . . the art
of empirical jurisprudence is cognate to him, although he may not
like it. No country, indeed, has produced more bitter complaints
and satires about the legal profession than England (Weber, tr.
1978:890–1).

In 1789, the representatives of the French people resolved '. . . to set
forth in a solemn declaration the natural, inalienable, and sacred
rights of man . . .'. These rights, the preservation of which was the
'aim of every political association', were 'liberty, property, security,
and resistance to oppression.' That sometime law student, Karl Marx,
was later to complain that this based the right of man to liberty 'not on
the association of man with man, but on the separation of man from
man' (tr. 1975:162). 'None of the so-called rights of man . . . go
beyond egoistic man . . . separated from the community. In the rights
of man . . . society . . . appears as a framework external to the individuals, as a restriction of their original independence. The sole bond
holding them together is natural necessity, need and private interest,
the preservation of their property and their egoistic selves'
(tr. 1975:164). Marx never departed from the conviction that the
abolition of private property (and the 'smashing', as Lenin was to call
it, of the state) were crucial for human emancipation and genuine
community, the key to unlocking the chains of the present. But what
is 'property', which, under two banners of freedom, now divides the
world into opposed camps?

If any social group is to exist as such, there have to be some shared understandings as to how access to things in general, and to scarce valued resources in particular, is to be arranged. To use the legal distinction, there is always a difference between a person's acquisition of physical control over a thing and the common recognition, the shared understanding, that he or she rather than anyone else 'should' have the thing. This much is true of even the remotest groups of hunter-gatherers, where relations between men and things are primarily geared towards consumption. Observers detect clear understandings how food, once gathered, should be consumed, about how larger game animals should be divided up. Among the Hadza of what is now Tanzania, for example, only adult males may consume certain parts of game animals; and a hunter is expected to provide meat for the mother of the woman with whom he lives (Woodburn, 1972). In even the simplest societies, therefore, a set of norms surrounds the consumption of valued scarce resources, norms concerned not just with what kinds of things should or should not be consumed, but with who can consume particular things over which control has been assumed.

Possession among hunter-gatherers of the most important thing – food – is of necessity transient and geared to regimes of consumption. In groups which are organised around stock-herding the position is transformed. The accent is no longer confined to the distribution and closely connected consumption of valued things, but shifts to their conservation and management through time. The element of time is decisive here, since the timespan over which people remain in control of certain things is greatly increased, and with it the degree of control which is required. The bush from which hunter-gatherers have picked today's nuts or berries can be forgotten until, with the cycle of the seasons, a new growth appears. A herd of goats, by contrast, demands closer and more constant attention. Assembling a herd of animals makes people think and reach understandings about what it means to have things in a way that a regime geared exclusively to distribution and consumption does not.

The practice of agriculture, of settled cultivation of land, effects further changes in how it is possible to think, because land poses most sharply and insistently the question of the relation between men and things. If you lose your ring or your cow, or have it taken from you, you may not be able to find it. Nor will it be obvious in most cases to someone encountering the thief that the thing in his possession is not his. Land stays put; most people remember where they were born and where they have lived. If someone takes your land, you must know unless you have moved on and abandoned it, because to take it he must be there and if he is there you cannot be. Settled cultivation forces people to think more intensely about what it means to have things, and about what things 'mean' in terms of relations between human beings.

Land also permits infinite degrees of intensity of exploitation, depending upon the technological capacities of a society, whether for grazing, growing crops, or building. Land is also continuous: it raises the question of boundaries, of where my land begins and yours stops. And your use of your land – or what you do on your land – may interfere with my enjoyment of my land – or my ability to enjoy peace and quiet when I am at home. Even if these disturbances arise from your use of or failure to control a chattel that belongs to you, it is our physical contiguity resulting from our respective occupancies of land which makes it possible for you to disturb me. If your music keeps me awake at night, or your goat eats my tomatoes, the conflict between us is not just a conflict between people but a conflict mediated by property in land, a conflict between landowners or occupiers of land.

A general human and social condition, then, is being delineated. In any culture, there must be some conception of right ways to allocate resources. There must be ideas about who can properly act in a given way in relation to a particular resource. In other words, there must be ideas about relations between men as well as ideas about the relations between men and things. And land focuses the collective mind on these questions.

This general condition does not mean that every society has an idea of ownership or 'private property', in the sense that 'This goat is mine' or 'This is my field' means that I have exclusive access to it. It is possible for no one to think in terms of 'my goat' or 'my field' at all. But in all societies the different normative problems which the existence of the goat and the field presents for the members must be resolved. Who can manage the goat undisturbed, who can have its milk, its offspring, or the goat itself to eat, and what is to happen when the present holder dies? The same is true of land: who is responsible for its management, who may cultivate it, who can take the harvest and what difference will the death of human beings make to the answers to these questions. All of them flow from the very nature of the relation between men in society and goats or land, and answers to these questions are invariably found.

This does not mean that people sit down and reach express agreement on these matters. How the allocation rules were arrived at may be unknown to the present members of the group, of no interest to them, and impossible for the observer to ascertain. Secondly, nothing that has been said requires the presence of 'government' if by that is meant differentiated agencies attempting to police resource allocation. (Whether government should be so conceived is another matter.) Ethnography abounds with examples of communities which clearly have shared ideas about how resources should be allocated, and where people appear to act regularly in conformity to those ideas, but where there are no specialised agencies to oversee how resources are managed or controlled. Where states exist, we must always bear in mind the differences which may occur between the 'spontaneous' or almost unconscious reproduction of norms within social groups and their conscious and often calculative production in the official systems of the modern state.

The majority of states have assumed a rather limited number of functions in relation to property. In the past, these were largely undifferentiated, whereas today they belong to distinct 'fields' of activity and expertise. First and foremost, perhaps, in the modern world, we think of the state as an organised system charged with redistributing resources. States impose taxes in various forms and the revenues of these taxes are used to provide benefits, in the form either of services (health, education) or cash (welfare benefits, food stamps etc.). Taxation, however, is perhaps the most primordial form of the relation between a state and its citizens, in which resources are exacted for the waging of war or the staging of spectacles. Many of the earliest pressures to establish 'good government' and to define property at the same time are rooted in royal searches for revenue and the resistance of loyal subjects.

A second function of the state has been to police the circulation of things. Governments of the past often sought to control the movement of things within, or in and out of, the territories they claimed to control, to maximize the amount of wealth within the territory and thus the resources available for fighting wars. (For a different view, see Ekelund and Tollision, 1981.) Today, this has become a branch of international trade, subsumed within the intricacies of the world economy. Governments in the past also sought to regulate consumption, by enacting 'sumptuary legislation', to regulate, for example, the wearing of certain types of clothing. Such forms of regulation were aimed principally at preserving gradations of rank in a stratified society, at regulating the signification or communication of status through things, through the clothes which people wore. Even the once common prohibition upon aliens owning land, which survives in some countries even today, was largely rooted in the general normative overlay upon the relation between people and things, in which 'property' was really a social relation between people, a relation mediated by the presence of things. Perhaps only the modern world has experienced a purely 'economic', 'rational' approach to the planned regulation of consumption, in the form, for example, of war rationing.

The state is just one mechanism through which resources can be allocated in a society, and not necessarily the most effective or efficient one at that. But one difference which the emergence of the state may make is that it generates a tendency to talk about 'oughts' (which may or may not from a normative point of view encapsulate shared understandings) in terms of 'rights'. It is one thing to say that in most societies the relation between men and things is moralised so that certain modes of behaviour can be characterised indigenously as right or wrong. Something seems to change when 'right' is turned into a substantive noun, when 'a' right becomes something which one can 'have'. What might be suggested is that even if the idea of property does not presuppose a state, the idea of having rights to property, as opposed to there simply being right ways of dealing with things, does.

Here we reach a central paradox. On the one hand, the existence of sovereign power seems to be a precondition for the existence of 'property' (as opposed to things and the vague set of normative understandings attached to certain things). On the other hand, the existence or protection of sovereign power has always been seen as presenting a problem for property. Given sovereign power, how can it be prevented from taking the very property which it has constituted? Most ideas of constitutionality have their origin in this problem.

Our primary concern here, however, is with the role of government in providing a facility for the resolution of disputes about the ownership or use of things. Here, one must distinguish the state's role in relation to taking – and, in particular, theft – from its role in relation to the transfer of property from one person to another. Much of this book is concerned with how lawyers formalised this process of transfer, especially in relation to landownership, and with the consequences which flow from this for understanding English property law.

What emerges from this discussion is that the exploration of the relationship between people and things, property and ownership, requires the formulation of a number of precise questions in place of the large question 'What is Property?' These are now listed, though only some can be pursued in this book, since its central concern is not 'property' in general, but property law as English lawyers understand it.

1. How far is the management or administration of a thing distinguished from its enjoyment such that the two are located in different groups or individuals?

2. In what kind of units is management or enjoyment located? To what extent is enjoyment exclusive to a particular person, kinship group or territorial unit, to take the most obvious possibilities?

3. To what extent do those who manage or enjoy things have freedom of disposition over them?

4. What are the principal means through which access to and control over things is acquired?

5. What, if any, are the arrangements for intergenerational transmission of things?

6. To what extent are there institutions within the group or external to it which are explicitly concerned with policing resource management and enjoyment?

Only close scrutiny of the arrangements and thought patterns discernible in a particular culture enables observers to answer these questions. It is simply wrong to suppose that they can usefully be asked in general terms which transcend the particularities of different societies.

These are essentially sociological questions. The question of property can be posed in another register, that of political theory. Within this tradition, as Ryan has emphasised, there are two distinct inflections. In one, property is emblematic of self-development. In the other, property is conceived instrumentally. Both are concerned, at root, with the justification of property, and both, it should be added, can be seen as responses to the problem posed by property within the tradition of Christian thought, with its ethic of the renunciation of the things of this world. In brief, instrumentalism justifies property in terms of efficiency. It links work and property in a particular way. Property is a means to an end, the efficient exploitation of the natural resources of the world.

> Since ownership or non-ownership has no intrinsic significance for individuals, it must be an instrumental question whether the recognition and enforcement of private property rights in land, raw materials and the produced means of production, yields social benefits. If property rights are an indispensable condition of a good life, for extrinsic reasons; if only some such system encourages adequate levels of thrift and effort; or if any alternative would have appalling political costs, then they are justified (Ryan, 1984: 9–10).

This view of the nature of property, Ryan suggests, was particularly pronounced in English political thought. As we stress throughout this book, it is strongly mirrored in English lawyers' fundamentally instrumentalist conception of their own role vis-à-vis property. The self-developmental perspective, by contrast, involved, first, the idea that 'there is, or can be, and certainly should be, something intrinsically satisfying about work; work is a characteristic form of human self-expression' (Ryan, 1984: 11). Secondly, this tradition treats the relationship between a man and what he owns as intrinsically significant, as more than a mere, instrumental means to an end. 'There is in the European tradition a concern for how work and ownership unilaterally create a world more thoroughly human and therefore a world more permeated with (or better able to do without) the divine plan that is hardly visible in British thinking' (ibid).

It is not suggested that English political thinking was less religious or more modern in the eighteenth century than in Europe. 'The patriarchal, hierarchical confessional state found its legal language not in rights, but in writs; its political language not in secret ballots, but in personal oaths' (Clark, 1985: 191–2).It is simply that the question of property fitted differently into two modes of thought about politics and about the nature of the relationship between rulers and ruled.

Many law students believe that property law – and land law in particular – is difficult. It is seen as obscure, complicated, hard to 'grasp', resistant to all but the keenest – or most persevering – intelligence. The main objective of this book is to explore the reasons for this reputation and, in doing so, to try to make the subject more accessible.

Perhaps the first problem is that it is not clear where the boundaries of the 'subject' are to be drawn. The boundaries of 'contract', 'tort' and 'crime' are relatively clear, whether these boundaries are drawn by law teachers for pedagogical purposes or by practitioners as a means of describing and differentiating their own activities. Secondly, even if it is uncontentious to assert that property law is concerned with the way in which the enjoyment and management of things is regulated, no internally coherent conceptual framework exists in which such rules are to be found. There is, in fact, no such thing as 'the law of property' in general. First and foremost, as we shall see, this is because the 'law' regarding land and the 'law' regarding other things have developed separately, and as a result, distinctive rules have grown up in regard to each. The legislature, the judiciary, lawyers in practice and academic lawyers all treat land as different from other things, so far as their respective engagements with or interests in the law of property are concerned. As we shall see, in 'land law' the central focus is upon the major statutes of 1925; the law relating to moveables is largely codified in the Sale of Goods Act 1893; in addition there is legislation dealing with 'specialised' areas such as patents and copyright.

Practitioners and academic lawyers work, for the most part, with a bifurcated literature: there are books on land law and books on personal property (or the sale of goods). The labour of writing a book on 'property law' is rarely undertaken.'[1] And unsurprisingly – law books largely determine the 'boundaries' of law courses – most law school curricula engage in a form of apartheid, keeping land law apart from what law there is relating to the ownership and disposal of other things. Indeed, the law relating to 'other things' tends to appear interstitially, in commercial law courses for example, as principally a set of problems thrown up in the law of contract. It is not presented as something fundamental to the way English lawyers think about property and therefore as something essential to understanding what, for the English lawyer, property means.

These factors make it difficult to provide a coherent presentation of how English lawyers think about something called 'property' in general. In this respect the common law stands in sharp contrast to the civil law jurisdictions of continental Europe, with their codified law modelled upon the example of Justinian.[2] As a result, there are no clearly defined external boundaries between property and other institutions of English private law; nor are there any authoritatively arranged internal subdivisions of the subject. There is no one 'text' which can serve as the starting point for the lawyer or the student of law, that can be used as the Institutes of Justinian were in the medieval universities. Moreover, the very project of codification pulls in the direction of theorisation, completeness and logical arrangement. Codes also often state rules in very general terms, partly in the interests of logical coherence, partly for more practical reasons. (The Napoleonic Code was produced at great speed, so its generality and relative brevity was more or less inevitable.) English law has not grown up in this way, but rather in a piecemeal, and leisurely, fashion.

The 'rules' we are trying to understand in this book have emerged over a long period of time as a result of the day-to-day activities of lawyers in their offices, devising mechanisms to give effect to the wishes of their clients, as a result of the accidents of litigation, and through legislative intervention from time to time, usually addressed to fairly narrowly defined problems which lawyers or judges have encountered in the course of their work. It follows that English law is often silent on matters which the professionals simply take for granted, and on matters of no practical importance which, if one was striving for completeness or logical arrangement, might need to be addressed.

So the upshot is that the word 'property' has no single, simple meaning for English lawyers if and when they care to examine the concepts which they use. This fact is not in itself a problem, though one consequence of it is that what political theorists or economists have to say about property can often diverge from the way lawyers talk about it. For our purposes, the point which cannot be emphasised enough, and we return to it below, is that lawyers' conceptualisations of 'property' grow out of the nature of lawyers' diverse involvements in the relation between men and things.

So, to summarise, lawyers encounter property in the following contexts. First, they are concerned with the preparation of written instruments dealing with title (essentially to do with questions of proof and mechanisms of transfer). As we shall see, the bulk of lawyers' work is of this character, which provides the key to what 'formalism' really means in the English legal system. Secondly, lawyers service and adjudicate upon disputes concerning property.

In these contexts, one can see lawyers' 'learning' as so many tools of the trade, as concepts and categories within which to present the argument and the decision. Here, it is important not to run together the tools with the uses to which they are put; a limited range of tools may be set to work in widely divergent dispute contexts. Secondly, there is a range of disputes concerning the use of property. Lawyers have come to elaborate a range of rights to property, and to land in particular, which provides a framework within which such disputes about land use can be processed.

Against this background, we have chosen to centre our discussion around land, and to deal much more briefly with property in other things, for several reasons. First, as already indicated, land law is conventionally taught and studied as a subject in its own right, and our principal task here is to assist the student embarking upon that rather arduous course of study. Secondly, as we have said, lawyers themselves have long treated land – and transactions involving land – as different from transactions involving other things. The legal regimes regarding other things are largely to be found in the law of contract and the remedies for protecting or asserting claims to other things are a branch of the law of tort. Land has its own regime(s). It is obvious even to the layman that buying a house is a much more elaborate – and again arduous, even stressful – affair than buying a car.

Considerable difficulties remain even if we abandon the attempt to deal with 'property' in general and direct most of our energy to trying to understand land law. What is land law about? Most teachers would no doubt reply that it is about learning a set of rules, whether or not these rules should be set in their 'context', whatever that means, and whether or not the exposition of these rules should be merely 'positive', just saying what they are, or evaluative, subjecting them to a 'critique' developed from some perspective or other. But even if one accepts one of these versions of the pedagogical enterprise, at whom are these rules to be taken to be targeted? Are we concerned with what judges do in court, with what lawyers do in the office, or with what people do in life?

There is, in England, no securely established tradition of legal education so far as the common law is concerned. In the past, lawyers learnt what they needed to know principally by sitting in courts, chambers and offices, by listening, watching, helping out and, finally, by trial and error. It is probably more like that even today than most are prepared to admit. The leading textbooks focus upon the decisions of the superior courts, as if they are enunciating a set of normative rules. This means that the practical character of land law is either ignored or taken for granted, and not made explicit for the reader. The heart of the matter – the work of conveyancers in their offices, preparing documents of transfer, drafting wills and so on – is largely treated as peripheral to the exposition of 'principle'. This means that 'land law' is presented in something of a vacuum, since its ground is this paperwork which takes place in the office and which is later worked over, in one way or another, by judges and legislators when 'problems' emerge.

In the standard texts, as a result, it is hard if not impossible for the student to tell the wood from the trees, to tell what is a difficult question and what is not, what is a minor quirk of history which never posed any practical difficulty and so could be left undisturbed, from what is a major mess too complex for anyone adequately to resolve. However, even if the practical context, when supplied, can make some matters less mysterious, it is in and of itself insufficient. The closer one examines it, the more its highly instrumental character comes into view. It then becomes necessary to ask to what ends the instruments are being put. This requires a much wider appreciation of the 'context' of property law. Perhaps most important of all, it requires one to explore the assumptions, the ideas which are taken for granted, the 'unsaid', which makes what is said intelligible to the actors at the time – the owners of property, their lawyers and their judges – and which needs to be drawn out if we as observers are to understand what is going on. Without this 'context of the obvious', a highly distorted reading of the legal material is likely to result.

This point is elaborated further below. Before doing so, we must note some further barriers to understanding which are at least relatively easy to state. The first is mainly of historical significance, but it remains fundamental to understanding the subject even today. This is what lawyers call the '1925 legislation'.

The study of land law in modern England very largely defines its boundaries with reference to the matters at which this legislation was aimed. The study of land law, in other words, is principally a gloss or commentary upon these statutory texts and the decisions which have interpreted them. For this reason, it will be necessary in certain parts of this book to discuss explicitly how judicial interpretation should proceed in the face of a body of statutory material of such length, complexity, and, by the practical standards of English lawyers, longevity.

Given the centrality of this legislation to the study of land law, it is imperative for the student to grasp that much of its framework was constructed with the objective of simplifying certain aspects of the legal regimes governing the landed estates of the past, and that the problems to which the legislation was addressed have little relevance in the modern world of owner-occupation of houses and flats. As we shall see, a number of important difficulties flow from this fact of historical change.

The second barrier in the way of a coherent presentation, again principally of historical significance, is no less fundamental. This is the division between 'law' and 'equity'. There were, as again we shall see in more detail later, for much of the history of English law, two types of courts proceeding in some measure independently, throwing up different guidelines, principles, rules and remedies, even if neither proceeded in a vacuum and each was, for many centuries, cognisant of the practices of the other. The 'trust' (see Chapter 4) is a good, and perhaps the most important, example of this jurisdictional divide. It remains a fact that much legal energy was devoted to working out the relationship – largely in jurisdictional terms – between these two bodies of law, and that, even though these two streams of law, if they can be so described, are now administered in every court, 'history' has left a deep imprint upon the contemporary fabric in this respect. As a result, any overall outline of the English law of property cannot but dart to and fro between 'law' and 'equity', each with its own organising conceptual principles, at the expense of overall coherence.

The final, more technical, barrier to a coherent exposition of the land law is that the 1925 legislation left us with two distinct schemes regulating transfer of title to land. While one of these schemes – registered conveyancing – was, at least as it was publicly presented (cf. Offer, 1977), designed to replace the other – unregistered conveyancing – this process is still incomplete today. As a result, the student of land law has to master two different regimes of land law, which differ from each other, as we shall see, in some important ways.

The principal obstacles to the understanding of land law have now been introduced. We must now examine more closely the central question outlined above: what is it all about? Is it about what judges do in court? Clearly some of it is. Is it about what lawyers do in their offices? Clearly, some of it is about this as well. Such affirmative answers throw up another question. If different parts of what we classify as land law concern one or other of these activities, what is the relationship between these activities, and what does this mean for the study of land law? The standard textbooks give pride of place to the judges and treat them as if their main concern is with the formulation or interpretation of rules, or the development of The Law. One thing which this can obscure is the simple possibility that judges may often be indifferent to the outcome of the disputes upon which they have to decide.

Moreover, the construction of the pedagogical agenda around more or less heroic judges slotted in to a narrative of 'development' can obscure the primacy of what lawyers do in their offices, preparing documents which serve as instruments to achieve a client's wishes, documents which, it is hoped, will not attract the scrutiny of a judge at some later time. These are the conveyances and deeds of transfer which transfer property and regulate its use, the wills and trusts which channel property through the generations within a family and are designed to preserve it from the depredations of the taxman. To prepare these documents, lawyers resort to verbal formulae – to forms of words – which have worked in the past, recycling and adapting them to meet the needs of the present, but with no particular concern to modernise the language or prune away the sometimes florid or redundant expressions inherited from the past.

This level of activity, which constitutes such a large part of land law, gives rise to a second point. When lawyers are trying to achieve a given result for their client, they often encounter a number of alternative ways of reaching it. Where a particular formula has proved reliable in the past, there is no reason not to use it again, and its use becomes a matter of routine. But if at some point it shows signs of running into difficulty, for example because of some accident of litigation, it may well be discarded in favour of an alternative. The practice of law is about how to do things, how to achieve results. Where one formula appears problematic, you resort to a functional equivalent.

The important point for now is that we should not exaggerate the importance of judges. The driving force in the history of land law has been the activity of conveyancers. Their expertise was essentially formulaic, and remains so in large measure today. The role of the judge must be seen against the background of this work of conveyancers. For the most part, the judge comes on the scene only in those relatively rare cases where things go 'wrong', and then as a reader of formulae, for the most part, rather than as an interpreter of rules. The judge's role is thus responsive; his principal task is to state the effect of the formulae in the event of a dispute. It is this relationship too which helps to explain the often repeated advice that the Bench should defer to conveyancing opinion. If conveyancing practice has proceeded for a period of time on the basis that a particular formula has a particular legal effect, so that possibly hundreds of conveyances, wills or settlements have been drawn up on that basis, there is obviously strong pressure on a judge in the course of litigation to accept the interpretation of the conveyancers.

In the area of land law at least, these factors put in question the adequacy of viewing judges as 'activists', whose role is to 'develop' the law. The job of an English judge is to resolve disputes, in the particular sense of deciding, as between the contestants before him, who will win and who will lose. Once this is done, the judge then has to draw up orders so that everyone knows what they must do when they go away from court. Judges are not there to develop the law. One difficulty the law student encounters is that the law books and law review articles are written in an idiom in which judges are cast as legislators whom it is appropriate to applaud or condemn in terms of their sloth or vigour in reforming or refurbishing the law. The point here is not that law reform is a good or bad thing; simply that this kind of work is not, for the most part, what judges do. If we mislead ourselves into supposing that this is what they do when it is not, we may find difficulty working out what judges really do.

Judging in England is a practical activity. Moreover, going by what most judges do rather than what they say, one of the most important aspects of that activity concerns keeping the litigation process under control. And more than anything, this means keeping control over the volume of private litigation. One consequence of this is that however bizarre or obscure or antiquated a rule is, there is no incentive to change it unless it causes inconvenience in a practical sense. In other words, real, living law may diverge from what, in a theoretical sense, could be said to be law. There are two basic, and irritating, points for the student of property law: lawyers work with what is to hand, however antique the materials may be, and some rules of law survive, remain part of the repertoire, long after they have been 'used' in any practical sense.

Judicial involvement in the development of land law thus takes place, for the most part, through the two-way communication of judges with lawyers. A lawyer tries to do something; in a dispute or just a hearing (eg. probate: in this area, not everything is a genuine dispute) a judge says it has failed; the lawyers then look for another way of achieving the same result, and so on. Much the same can be said about the construction of pleadings and the business of oral argument by barristers before judges: the barrister searches for alternative ways of presenting the case, the judge chooses between them.

This opportunistic resort to functional equivalents can make things seem more complicated than they really are. In the area of what is commonly called the 'family home', there are five or six ways of arguing and holding that a home owner will not be allowed to evict someone living in the home on an informal basis. From a conceptual point of view, some of these seem very different from the others; in a functional sense, they achieve the same result, and the choice between these concepts, for the purpose of giving a legal interpretation of everyday facts, seems arbitrary – a matter of personal preference or terminological fashion.

This suggests that the 'formalism' of which judges are sometimes accused is somewhat different in character from the way it is commonly presented. What most English scholars mean by formalism goes something like this. Once upon a time, when faced with a dispute, judges evaluated the merits of the issues as they saw them. For example, where the argument was about whether an agreement for a sale should be enforced by the court, the judge would hear argument about whether the price was just, and if he concluded that it was not, would refuse to enforce it. Formalism is associated in most people's minds with a progressive refusal by judges to adopt this sort of attitude. Instead, the 'formalist' judge asks simply whether certain general rules of contract formation have been complied with and leaves it at that. The link between this alleged development and an ideology of legal certainty is also treated as obvious: the judge who evaluates is being 'subjective' and therefore acting unpredictably. Even if barristers who appear before him regularly can predict how he is likely to respond in the event of a dispute, this kind of predictability falls far short, it is said, of the kind of certainty which a legal system must provide. First, because the predictions of counsel such as they may be are necessarily based on their personal knowledge and practical experience of the individual judge in action. Secondly, because the sort of certainty which is expected is one that you can have irrespective of the particular judge you end up before if you have a dispute. If the consequences of a transaction are to be knowable in advance, which is what certainty is taken most of the time to mean, they must not depend on 'subjective' factors but on objective ones that transcend individuals. From this it is a short step to saying that the fundamental characteristic of the judicial role is the negotiation of the tension between certainty and fairness. Some lean in one direction, others in the other, but such leaning is the name of the game. Every received wisdom contains some grain of truth. But most of the time, this so-called fundamental tension between certainty and fairness is not in issue. That is to say, most of the time judges are formalists, and for reasons connected with a need for certainty, but neither the formalism nor the idea of certainty are the ones we have so far described.

28

The formalism of the conventional wisdom is a formalism of rule-finding. This in two senses: first, to use the Weberian categories, that either a concrete balancing of the interests of contestants or a self-conscious evaluation of the merits with reference to some code of values is systematically excluded from the adjudicative process. Secondly and consequentially, that judicial decision-making is a matter of finding, following, or adapting rules, where the aims of consistency and logical coherence are paramount, and considerations of policy are not permitted to provide decision-making criteria. Judges themselves play along with this caricature because it is convenient. But in fact it is just one of the best kept secrets of the British establishment that this is not what judges do at all.

This does not mean that everything they do is 'policy', if that word, also overfamiliar to law students, has any meaning. Most of the time, English formalism means not the formalism of a rule-finder but that of a reader. The reading process which lawyers call rather grandly 'construction' lies at the heart of English Formalism. The developmental dynamic of property law, viewed over time, is largely a tension between strategies of construction and the refinement of classificatory frameworks in or through which to fit interpretations.

We are now in a position to return to the question of 'rules'. It has already been emphasised that both the work of judges in court and of lawyers in the office must be kept in play if we seek to understand land law. But is there any general sense in which the 'rules' concerned with the process of adjudication are different from those concerned with the office work of lawyers? Of course in preparing the requisite documents for the transfer of land, lawyers must take some account of the rules with which judges are presented when they deal with standard texts. So, to take an example, a lawyer wishing to draft a legally binding long lease must make sure that the form which he or she uses is one recognised by the courts as a 'deed'. But other kinds of statements are encountered in the books, which seem a bit like 'rules', and which are equally important to the work which lawyers do.

Take for example the proposition: 'Every well-drawn lease should contain an express forfeiture clause.' As we shall see, this is the sort of thing a solicitor could do with knowing, though the standard forms he will acquire from a legal stationer are likely to contain such a clause anyway. There is no harm in this being known by a law student either, but he might take time out, if encouraged or permitted, to reflect on what sort of proposition it is. Is it a rule? Well, it is not a rule like a rule against rape or a rule requiring you to stop at a red light, or even, as we shall see, the rule contained in section 52 of the Law of Property Act 1925. It is a rule of 'good sense', a pragmatic rule first and foremost, for solicitors to follow in their offices. Legal education, as is well known, is in large measure the inculcation of this legal good sense. But precisely what could, perhaps should, be the object of scrutiny – a pragmatic rule in a practical environment – is passed by unnoticed. It is not, however, just a pragmatic rule; it may have a certain normative content. A solicitor who fails to include such a clause may not only be acting unwisely but at very least unprofessionally; possibly, in court-law terms, negligently.

Codification was, since the middle of the eighteenth century, and still is today in some countries of the Third World, an emblem of modernization, an explicit break with the customs and practices of the past. And this feature of codification meant that, in nineteenth-century France and Germany, jurisprudence divided into two opposing camps, those championing codification as the expression of 'reason', and those insisting that it must give expression to and embody the established customs and culture of the people or nation, which could only be known through 'history'. Property and, in particular, rules relating to the inheritance of property and its devolution through time, were often at the heart of this debate, because almost every society, however simple, has customary rules of some sort concerning these elementary questions, and the project of codification always poses the question of whether the code is to adopt or reject the traditional rules.

Property law in England underwent no such explicit break with the past, of the kind usually associated with the project of codification. This is usually taken to be the principal reason why the study of property law is difficult. Even its language bears the imprint of the past, a rag-bag of Norman–French, ecclesiastical Latin, and English archaisms. Property lawyers talk in an esoteric, peculiar language that seems radically divorced from the language of ordinary life.

What Is Property?

This is indeed one reason why property law seems inaccessible, and this inaccessibility does have important, negative, practical consequences. It is not satisfactory, as we shall see, that the language lawyers use to conceptualise home ownership today is unintelligible to the people who own the houses, or that people who own leases of flats do not understand what the words in the lease mean. But locating the difficulty of land law in its language can be misleading, or, at least, imprecise. If you read a legal judgement, modern or not so modern, there are a number of reasons why you may find it difficult to understand (assuming, as is not always the case, that what the judge says makes good 'legal sense'). Much of the time, what you think is a difficulty with the law is a difficulty getting to grips with the facts. This is because what underpins many, though not all, disputes about property is one or more property transactions, where the dispute is about some consequence or other of the transaction. The student's difficulty in understanding the transaction – its nature or its logic – causes difficulty in understanding the dispute which, in turn, leads to difficulty in understanding the decision. Very often, at the level of language, a judge's decision is written in relatively non-esoteric, 'ordinary' terms; but his account of the transaction is hard to follow. Why is this? Because commonly it is expressed in the language of the transaction itself. Much of property law, as we shall see in this book, is about what words mean, and the words in question are the words used by lawyers when they prepare transactions. And it is in the use by lawyers of words in transactions that the imprint of the past is most evident, and the barrier to understanding which flows from this fact most firmly in place. And it follows from this that to understand the subject, you need to understand the kinds of property transactions people enter into with which lawyers have been principally concerned, past and present. And you need to understand typical transactions of the past because, as we shall see, they have left their mark upon the present, not just on the vocabulary we have inherited but on the shape of the rules, on the way that they hang together, to the extent that they do.

So far it has been suggested that the past impinges upon the present by shaping the language, the categories, and some of the rules which lawyers use in property law. So we can understand the law better if we know something of this impingeing past, of why people behaved as they did, and of when they needed lawyers to help them do what they wanted to do. But one final point must be stressed in examining the impact of the past upon the fabric of English land law. Its impact has been on the terminology, the formulae, the organising structure of the rules, and to some extent the substantive content of particular 'settled' rules. It does not follow from this that English property lawyers are interested in or concerned with the past as such, in the manner of an historian. Quite the opposite is the case, and even the studied antiquarianism of some of the standard textbooks is no exception to this generalisation. Rather than, as with codification, the history of property law being sundered by a sudden break, English legal history is more a case of incremental drift, of changes which are often imperceptible precisely because English lawyers rarely take the past seriously, rarely approach it on its own terms. This means that change often appears as continuity.

To conclude, it must be emphasised that this blindness to 'history' or this incrementalism of the common law cannot be attributed simply to the large space afforded by the English legal system for judge-made law. Exactly the same stance, and drift, can be observed in the approach of the judiciary to the interpretation of statutes. By contrast with, say, the law of contract or the law of tort, a considerable part of the land law has long been statutory. In the modern world, this anti-historical attitude, as we shall see, is particularly well exemplified in a much-used slogan, 'the policy of 1925'. In this book, we take the view that, to understand the structure of the 1925 legislation, it is necessary to look seriously at the practices of the past; but this, it must be stressed, is something with which lawyers are rarely, if ever, concerned.

2

What Is Property Law?

An understanding of English property law requires close attention to the fundamental classificatory schemes which give shape and structure to the conceptual framework within which lawyers talk and think. These schemes are peculiar to lawyers and in that sense specialised. The distinctions contained in them, as we shall see, do not always correspond to the way people think about property in everyday life, or, indeed, to the way in which, in the modern world, other specialised ways of thinking, notably economics, define the nature of property. But the systems of classification within which lawyers work, like other systems of classification, rest on certain assumptions. These assumptions are not always made explicit in legal discourse, but when we examine them, it becomes clear that they diverge less from those held in everyday life than do the classifications erected upon the ground of these assumptions.

The central assumption is that 'private ownership' by 'individuals' is the normal way in which things are held. This concept of ownership is made up from three elements: the right to manage things, the right to enjoy or consume them, and the right to dispose of them during life or upon death. And the use of the term 'right' here indicates that at its core 'ownership' is not a way of conceptualising the relation between people and things but the relation between people (between owners and non-owners), a relation which is mediated by things. This last point is elaborated below.

These elements of ownership, it is essential to grasp, are treated by English lawyers as severable from each other. The right to manage a thing may be held by one person, the right to enjoy it by another, the right to dispose of it by a third. Equally, each of these elements of ownership may itself be fragmented in various ways. The right to manage, enjoy or dispose of a thing may be shared concurrently between several persons, or it may be split up over time, so that one

33

or more persons has the right at one time, another at a later time. As we shall see throughout this chapter and the chapters which follow, this fragmentation of the elements of ownership and the internal fragmentation of each element accounts for much of the 'complexity' which the student of property law encounters.

While the individual provides the 'model' or 'paradigm' of ownership, an 'owner' does not have to be an individual human being or a group of them. Commercial organisations can own property, as can public authorities. These are legal, non-natural persons and are treated as if they were human beings for the purpose of conceptualising their ownership of things: hence the 'trespassers will be prosecuted' signs commonly found outside a block of council flats. Nor is this idea of 'legal personality' constructed by analogy with the human being new; centuries ago, when a bishop died, lawyers had to work out what part of 'his' property belonged to him personally and what part belonged to the Bishopric such that it would pass to his successor in office. Equally, in this way, monasteries could accumulate vast wealth through gifts while the monks who ran them remained true to their vow of poverty.

English property law is permeated by a strong sense of 'individualism', and this is particularly true of the way it treats the devolution of property on death. It starts from the position that an individual owner has complete freedom to direct how his property should be distributed after he is dead, by contrast with most European systems, which start by guaranteeing certain rights of succession to the next generation, constraining freedom of testamentary disposition from the outset. Paradoxically, this added to the complexity of ownership through devices like dower (the common law's traditional provisions for widows) which mitigated testamentary freedom, and leaves its mark even today, where disinherited widows and dependants must invoke a modern statutory jurisdiction which enables the court to make a discretionary award from the deceased's estate in such circumstances.

English lawyers are not much given to 'idle' speculation, so that these assumptions function for the most part as an implicit ideology rather than an explicit theory. Indeed, the term 'owner' is most likely to be encountered when it is not at issue. When it is, lawyers are more inclined to use a different term, 'title'. In disputes concerning 'ownership' they do not ask or seek to show who is the owner in any absolute sense, but rather which of the disputants has a 'better' title to the thing at issue, ignoring the possibility that someone with a better claim than anyone in court may come forward in the future. Again, there seems a marked contrast here between the English approach and that of the civilian systems modelled on Roman law. Roman law defined explicitly what ownership (*dominium*) was, and had a specific, general remedy (*vindicatio*) through which it could be asserted in court.

Two classificatory schemes, which provide the English law of property with such structure as it has, must now be singled out for discussion. The first concerns how lawyers classify things themselves, and the consequences which flow from this. The second concerns how lawyers classify the range of rights one may hold in respect of things. But we must first examine the distinction between these two focal points of classification, in which 'rights' and 'things' appear to belong to two different levels of legal experience. The term 'property' is for the most part used by non-lawyers with unselfconscious ambiguity, its meaning slipping backwards and forwards between 'the thing itself' and the 'rights' a person has to the enjoyment of the thing. The difference between 'your car' and 'your rights' over it is not obvious to you most of the time as you go about your day-to-day affairs. You may never encounter the distinction at all unless someone steals the car and it finds its way through a chain of buyers and sellers into the hands of an innocent buyer who refuses to give it back when you trace the car to him.

The distinction is more obvious in other cases, for example, where you have an income interest in a capital fund. If you view the fund as the thing, then all you can say is that you have certain rights in respect of that fund – to be paid a certain percentage of its annual yield, for example. But further, we must note that in such circumstances, you can easily come to think of your rights in regard to the thing as a thing in itself, with which you can go to market, as it were, and trade. And if you think about debts or patents or copyright, 'things' which have no tangible existence, the difference between the thing itself and the right to the thing becomes even more obscure. But for lawyers, this distinction is fundamental and needs to be maintained if the fabric of property law is to be grasped. One further reason for the inaccessibility of property law to the student is that the distinction is not always clearly maintained in the words lawyers use themselves. For example, as we will see, lawyers often say 'land' when strictly they mean 'title to land'. Because lawyers, like anyone else, know what they really mean from the context in which they use a word, they often use shorthand forms of this sort. For the non-initiate, this can cause confusion, since it seems to undermine what they are told is fundamental. So a commentator should often add a marginal note; we say 'land' but 'strictly speaking' we mean 'title to land'.

At any rate, it is much easier to grasp English property law if we always bear in mind that transactions involving things are, for lawyers, 'strictly speaking', transactions involving rights to things. For the lawyer, what you have is rights not things. From this base line, as we shall see, lawyers go on for the most part to talk about such rights as if they were the things in respect of which these rights are operative.

THE CLASSIFICATION OF THINGS

Real property and personal property

Originally, the emergence of property law is linked to the growth of remedial assistance from the royal courts in particular. The transformation of land law into essentially a body of professional know-how relating to land transfer – i.e. conveyancing – is consequent upon and not antecedent to the process of dispute settlement. This needs to be borne in mind as we turn to what is usually supposed to be both a fundamental aspect of the English lawyer's way of thinking about property, viz., the distinction between rights to land and rights to other things, or between 'real' and 'personal' property.

The terms real and personal come from the Institutes of Justinian, the most important textbook after the Bible in the medieval universities of Europe. The Institutes were divided into four parts: Persons, Things, Obligations and Actions. As Maitland tells the story, the distinction between persons and things was first appropriated by medieval English lawyers to distinguish two types of remedy or judgement, real remedies by which a successful plaintiff recovers the thing claimed, and personal remedies where the value of the thing may be all that can be recovered. By the mid-thirteenth century, real remedies were available for the recovery of land, but, according to Bracton, moveables could not be recovered through a real action: '. . . by merely paying [the defendant] is discharged, whether the thing be forthcoming or no' (quoted Maitland, 1932: 368). This is not surprising in the Middle Ages, Maitland suggests, since most chattels were perishable and of a kind where it would be straightforward enough to assess the value of the thing; '. . . if the plaintiff got the [price] of his ox he got what would do as well as his ox' (ibid).

Maitland saw this as the ('much to be regretted') origin of 'all our talk' about real and personal property. First, an action comes to be treated as 'real' if you get possession of land from the court, as 'personal' if you get damages and 'mixed' if you get both. This in turn led lawyers in time to distinguish 'things real' and 'things personal'.

Whatever the historical origins of the distinction between real and personal property, and its consequences good or bad for analytical jurisprudence, it is worth recalling at this stage one central point made in the introduction. Lawyers' conceptualisations of property grow out from the nature of lawyers' involvements in the relations between men and things. In the case of chattels, it is still the case today that their involvement is principally concerned with the litigation process. In the case of land, such involvement is subsidiary and subordinated to their involvement in the process of the management of land transfer. So the law of personal property remains primarily remedial in character, while land law is in essence structured around conveyancing.

Choses in action

Traditionally, if very long ago, the distinction between real and personal property did correspond to a fairly straightforward scheme of things, in particular to the distinction between immoveable and moveable property. In the modern law, however, perhaps the best we can suggest is that personal property means those rights which approximate to what lawyers mean by property which are not rights in land. Alongside this distinction between the categories of 'land' and 'moveables' is a further distinction between rights in tangible and intangible property. Thus a right of way over land is 'intangible': you can touch your field but not your right to walk across someone else's. Rights in real property are thus internally divided into rights to corporeal (tangible) and incorporeal (intangible) things.

An analogous internal subdivision is made in the category of personal property, but its significance, as we shall now see, is slightly different. Things which have a tangible physical existence – cars, books, animals – comprise what lawyers mean much of the time by 'personal property'. But rights to intangible personal property have also come to be recognised, especially in modern times, by lawyers. They call such rights 'choses in action'. This means that these are things ('choses') whose ultimate 'thingness' resides in the owner's ability to bring an action in court, rather than in a person's ability to take physical possession of the thing in which he has the right. You can reclaim a book or a cow that belongs to you by regaining physical control of it. But if someone interferes with intangible personal property, you can only bring a legal action to stop the interference and obtain financial compensation; you cannot take it back because it has no physical existence. Examples of such intangibles are forms of industrial and intellectual property such as patents, trade marks, names and copyrights. Rights of this kind have the character of property insofar as they endure, within the limits laid down by law, against a wide range of people, and are capable of retaining their value and enforceability in the hands of the heirs of the initial holder, and can be passed on through sale or gift to others, who, through the transfer, acquire equal rights. These all provide examples, in the strongest sense, of rights which lawyers treat as things, where, by contrast with the ownership of tangibles, there is no 'thing' which can serve as shorthand to describe the right to the thing in question.

Certain types of debt or claims to money owed are also classified as choses in action and thus as property rights. Here the paradigm case is the right to repayment of borrowed money, like a bank loan. Also in this category are contractual obligations to pay a fixed sum of money, as when you agree to pay £90 to a garage to have a new clutch put in your car, or to provide agreed quantities of specific goods, like a case of a particular claret. The duty of an executor to pay a sum of money to a legatee is another example, the will endowing the legatee with rights conferring, inter alia, the possibility of passing on to another what he has inherited.

The long-established recognition of the transmissibility of rights to enforce debts makes the borderline between what English lawyers treat as property and what they treat as contract or as personal wrongs unclear. Some monetary claims, such as damages for libel or for personal injuries cannot be transferred, cannot be brought within the scheme of choses in action. This is sometimes said to be because of the indefinite and open-ended nature of such monetary claims; that unliquidated damages are at large until a compensatory figure is arrived at in the legal process. But other jurisdictions manage such questions differently, and permit transferability in such contexts. Negotiable instruments and money are also rights treated as things, and, as a result, as property. As such, they differ from the older and superficially analogous category of intangibles in land law, which, as we see below, are largely property rights only insofar as they can be annexed to tangible property, and are not recognised as independently transmissible property rights.

PERSONAL RIGHTS AND PROPERTY RIGHTS

A further fundamental distinction embedded in the conceptual framework of English property law, which, at the same time, is only rarely articulated, comes to the surface when lawyers try to conceptualise the enjoyment and management of things. This is the distinction between those rights or interests which lawyers treat as 'property' from those which they do not. This distinction too is not straightforward. What can be suggested is that so far as English law does contain a core idea of what a 'property right' means, that idea involves the combination of two essential elements, durability and transmissibility. Property rights are durable in the sense that the present holder of the right can defend it over time against a range of other people, including the person from whom he obtained the right. They are transmissible in the sense that the holder can pass them on to other people. Either or both of these qualities may be considerably restricted (such restrictions are considered below) but the right is still conceptualised as a property right. Only if neither attribute is present will lawyers not speak of a property right.

There are two senses in which a right can be regarded as 'personal' by lawyers. It may be personal in the sense that the right is held only against a particular person. So if such a right relates to the use of that person's land, it will not endure should the land pass into other hands. Traditionally, this was the case where a 'licence' was enshrined in a contract. Secondly, a right may be personal in that it is exercisable only by the person who has the right, and is not transmissible by him to anyone else.

In the social world, this legal distinction is not always observable in the use which people make of things. Consider the following example. You see that a neighbour has begun to drive his cattle across a field, which you have always assumed does not belong to him, in order to graze them on common land which lies on the other side. To a lawyer, this observable fact drawn from every day life might mean a number of different things. Your neighbour might simply be a trespasser; but if not, if his presence on the land was 'lawful', a lawyer could explain what you saw in several ways. Your neighbour might have a simple permission, a 'licence', a personal right which operated in his favour and only in his favour, a right enforceable only against the present owner of the land, which the owner might be able to terminate or revoke at any time. Alternatively, a lawyer might say that your neighbour had a property right, an 'easement', a right of way which he could pass on to anyone who bought his land in the future, a right which could be enforced against anyone who later bought the land over which the right of way operated. Yet again, of course, the explanation might be that your neighbour had bought or leased the stretch of land from the person you thought owned it. Exactly how a lawyer would arrive at one or other of these interpretations of what for the non-lawyer is one observable fact is examined later in this chapter and in the one which follows.

With some kinds of property rights, transmissibility appears to be the decisive element which distinguishes such rights from personal rights. This is the case with choses in action. A debt is classifiable as a property right in that it can be transferred by the creditor to someone else who is then the person to enforce the obligation. Such a right can be compared with the right to claim compensation for a personal injury, arising, say, from a car accident, which is not transferable. There is no magic in this distinction, and in some jurisdictions, personal injuries claims are transferable.

At the end of the day, faced with observable facts of the kind in our example above, it is for judges to decide which legal category best expresses the 'true' nature of the arrangement between the parties, to say what the transaction 'really' means in legal terms. But the history of English property law can largely be read as an attempt to render this interpretative process unnecessary, pre-empting the need for interpretation by formalising the nature of the arrangement in advance. At worst, because no one likes litigation, this displaces the process of interpretation from making legal sense of what people do in social life, of 'facts', to making sense of words on the page which have been written by lawyers. At best, it renders disputes about 'meaning' unnecessary or impossible, because lawyers have used verbal formulae which have become standard, the meaning of which is beyond dispute in a court of law. We return to the significance of this in the final chapter.

OWNERSHIP AND ENGLISH LAW

Although, as we have seen, a concept of 'ownership' – the idea that a person can acquire secure, exclusive enjoyment of a thing and transmit it to another – underpins the English law of property, lawyers rarely talk explicitly in these terms. Rarely in the literature do we encounter discussions which compare, in length or subtlety, with those of *dominium* in Roman law, nor does English legislation endow ownership with specific characteristics and consequences in the manner of the civilian codes. Instead, we must examine a cluster of techniques which English lawyers have developed over a long period of time for processing disputes concerning things. Some of these techniques can be presented as exemplifying a 'principle', but even these, as we shall see, are in fact abbreviated statements of how the business of litigation over things has been managed in the English courts.

Three central elements are combined here. First, 'title' is treated as a relative notion, which is shorthand for saying that in a dispute over a thing, English courts confine themselves to asking who, as between the parties in court, has the better title. A further manifestation of this principle of relativity, as we shall see, is the effective absence of special remedies for owners as compared with those available to people with lesser claims to things. Relativity is complemented by two further principles. First, a time limit is placed on the availability of remedies for the recovery of things. Secondly, subject to these

41

time limits, the logic of relativity of title has the effect of protecting the integrity of a good title against subsequent dealings with a thing inconsistent with that title. Each of these must now be examined.

Relativity of title

In Roman law, title and ownership were not distinguished. Rather, ownership and lesser rights were clearly differentiated. Separate remedies were available for the assertion before a tribunal of what were considered to be qualitatively different kinds of claims. As the English system developed, however, the distinction was blurred, as people who in practical terms were asserting ownership rights – and who presumably thought of themselves as the owner of the thing in question – made use, procedurally, of remedial avenues which were equally available to people making less ambitious claims.

The fulcrum of the English system of remedies is possession rather than ownership. If you pick up a jewel in the street, and someone takes it from you and will not give it back, you can take him to court and recover its full value, even though it is obvious that a third person has a better title to the jewel than either of you. The person who took the jewel from you cannot defeat your claim by pointing to the defects in your title. He must pay you the full value of the thing, not some lesser sum reflecting your 'merely' possessory title. Your earlier possession suffices. The 'true owner' asserts his rights in exactly the same way. In terms of the conceptual structure of English property law, the distinction between 'true ownership' and merely possessory title is, at core, the difference between an earlier and a later taking of possession.

In the same way, if you hire someone's car, and a third person crashes into it and destroys it, you can recover its full value from him (or his insurance company), even though you have only hired it. Indeed, the logic of the English approach would seem to dictate – though there is no authority on the point – that the position would be the same even if the claimant was a thief. Thus, if you steal a car, and someone damages it, you could still recover in full against him. Your theft is no defence as far as he is concerned. The fact that you are a thief does mean that the person from whom you stole the car can claim its value from you if he catches up with you, and, of course, you might face criminal charges. But none of this helps the person who crashed into you.

In each of these examples, the earlier possession of the claimant enables him to succeed in court against the defendant. Even the 'true owner', when he claims, wins by virtue of his earlier possession or right to possession in a contest with a later comer. English law's conception of title is a relative one. The court listens to the claims of the parties who make an appearance and decides as between them which claim, compared or related to the other, is better. The potential or hypothetical claims of others are not relevant and are excluded from the proceedings. In short, the outcome of a dispute about rights to things depends on who shows up in court. And this means the possibility – however hypothetical or 'unreal' – of a series of law suits, with different winners on each occasion as people with successively better titles come forward and stake their claim.

Between the 'true owner' and the finder, another possible claimant must be introduced. So far we have talked about finding things in the street, that is, as lawyers put it, on a highway dedicated to the public, on a piece of land which nobody really owns although over which, in the modern world, various agencies of government have a range of responsibilities. But suppose you find something in somebody's garden, or in a shop, an airport lounge, or the forecourt of a garage. What, in other words, is the position if you find something on land which belongs to someone else? In comparing the claims of finder and landowner in this situation, the general principle is that the claim of the landowner is preferred. The person in possession of the land is treated as being in possession of the moveables on it. (This needs to be distinguished from the superficially cognate proposition that whatever is attached to the land – like a house or a fireplace in a house – forms part of it, a rule concerned with the transfer of title rather than its nature.) But there is a complicating factor in disputes between finders and landowners. This flows from the fact that many 'privately' owned places where people might find things are places to which the public has access, like shops, garage forecourts and airport lounges. In such places, the thing which is found may only recently have been left there, and the landowner may be unaware of its existence. Until recently, the 'better view' seemed to be that even in these circumstances the landowner would succeed against the finder, since his possession of the land was deemed to carry with it possession of things on it, so that, logically, his possession of the thing was earlier than that of the finder. However, a recent decision has held that where the public is permitted access to land, the occupier must take positive steps (like posting notices) to assert title over moveables left or lost by others on that land if he wishes to succeed against a finder.[3]

Behind the landowner, of course, is the true owner of the thing. As long as his claim is not barred by lapse of time, he will be able to recover his possession – or the value of the thing. But even longer chains of potential claimants can be imagined. You own a car. Someone steals it and then sells it to an honest buyer. He lends it to a friend and yet another person crashes into it and writes it off. Things can generate complex chains of legal as well as social relations between people.

This approach to title brings with it not only the possibility of a multiplicity of actions but also the possibility that a wrongdoer risks paying the full value of the thing to successive claimants. The recent Torts (Interference with Goods) Act 1977 addresses both problems. First, it requires plaintiffs to identify third parties who they believe may have an interest in the thing at issue. Such persons then have an opportunity to appear, and if, having been given the chance, they fail to do so, the court may deprive them of any claim against the defendant, to that extent preventing litigation arising in the future. Secondly, the Act requires anyone who is unjustly enriched through a chain of actions to reimburse someone who has paid out the value of the thing more than once. If, for example, I sell a ring which a finder has brought to me for valuation, the finder can recover in full against me, and I may have to pay again if the 'true' owner later appears. The Act requires that the finder, in these circumstances, must account to the true owner, who, in turn, becomes liable to reimburse me.

The same general approach is followed in relation to titles to land. Here, as we shall see, there are far more elaborate steps involved in its transfer than applies to most moveables, and, as a result, a sense of 'ownership' which seems more absolute than relative. But the documentary evidence of title to land which is normally required on a transfer of title is in principle irrelevant in a dispute where a plaintiff asserts an earlier possession against a later comer. So if a landowner who has acquired his title by transfer wishes to proceed against a squatter, his earlier possession is in principle a sufficient foundation for his claim, which does not need to be bolstered by his documents of title. Similarly, if one person enters land as a squatter, and is then displaced by another, new, squatter, the first squatter has the same recourse against the second as would the 'true owner'.

So how can a purchaser be sure that a claimant with a superior title will not emerge in the future?

Limitation of actions

Fundamentally, this problem is contained by limiting access to the courts and the remedies they provide through placing time limits on the commencement of actions. Access to the legal process is limited in an arbitrary way by statute, in terms of certain fixed periods of years, which, in brief, give you six years to claim a chattel or its value and twelve for land. Given these statutory periods, the crucial question, obviously, is when does time begin to run against the owner? In the case of moveable things, the answers are, from a legal point of view, relatively straightforward. If you lose something, time does not begin running, nor does time begin to run automatically if someone picks it up. It begins to run only when that person does something inconsistent with your own title, such as using the thing as his own. So it follows that time does not begin to run if an honest finder makes an attempt to trace the owner, but it begins to run at once in favour of a dishonest taker. Again, if you lend someone something, time starts from the moment he refuses to return it on request. Land admits of finer shades of occupancy. If you park your car on a piece of waste land, have you taken possession of it or do you have to build a fence around it before you can be said to possess it? The courts have, even in recent years, encountered some difficulty in defining what needs to have occurred before time starts to run against the landowner. What exactly must someone do if his possession of the land is to count as adverse?

Nemo dat quod non habet

We should now have a fairly clear idea about what lawyers mean when they talk about the quality of a given title. A title's quality is not something to be thought of in the abstract, but relatively, in relation to other titles. The quality of a title is judged by reference to its point of origin in time relative to that of others. The starting point is captured in a Latin maxim which can be paraphrased as 'the earlier in time, the stronger the right'. In theory, then, to investigate the quality of a title when a transfer is contemplated, you must look back and see how it first came about. This is often unnecessary in practice but it underpins how English lawyers think about the nature of title.

At this point we must introduce the third and final element of the conceptual structure, which expresses precisely this need to investigate back to the origin. It is expressed in a Latin tag: '*Nemo dat quod non habet*', 'No one gives what he does not have'. What this means is that you cannot transfer – by gift, sale, or on your death – better rights to a thing than you yourself have. We shall see that there are some exceptions to this principle. Like most exceptions to the rather exiguous number of general principles in this area, they arise because of practical convenience. Finally, we should note that once again we see, in this principle, the lawyer's overwhelming preoccupation with transfer. One might say that if 'relativity of title' is the slogan which encapsulates how courts go about their business, *nemo dat* sums up what happens in the lawyer's office.

If you find a jewel in the street and sell it, the buyer is as vulnerable to a claim from the true owner as you are yourself. Your title is no better than that of the person from whom you bought, and, as we have seen, that title originates in the taking of the thing itself. The combination of relativity of title, the limitation of actions, and *nemo dat* also means that, viewed strictly from the point of view of title rather than encumbrances on title (q.v.) there is no exact distinction between good and defective title in English law. Once again, we are back to the question of transfer of title. *Nemo dat* means that a squatter on land can pass on by a will what rights he has established just as the true owner can. The same transfer mechanisms are open to him. A daughter who takes under a will has as good a title as the original squatter who made the will. Even if she herself has never been present on the land, the will, coupled with the earlier possession, will enable her to succeed on the squatter's death against a later squatter who has taken over the land, provided she acts in time.[4]

If a squatter wants to sell his title, matters are different, but, as usual, for practical reasons. In accordance with *nemo dat*, a will simply involves passing on to successors whatever you have got. A lawyer is likely to enter the picture if buying and selling is involved, not because a lawyer must but because most people suppose it to be sensible to have a lawyer to act for them in such transactions. Of course it is sensible to have a lawyer as well if you want to make a will; but it is not essential and if a layman makes a will, that fact is taken into account in its construction where appropriate. By contrast, if you buy land and later get into dispute with your vendor, the courts will expect you to have taken the care expected of a land transfer specialist in investigating the quality of the title at your leisure. Traditionally, this is what distinguished land transactions from commercial transactions, where speed not leisure was crucial.

With selling a title, what is decisive is the state of professional opinion concerning the prerequisites of a safe or good title. Lawyers' predominant concern at this stage has been with incumbrances upon the title rather than the quality of the title itself, with one important exception, namely, fragmented title. Here, the focus is less upon the relative merits of a particular title vis-à-vis possible contenders, much more upon whether all the relevant interested parties who need to put their signatures to the documents of transfer have been ascertained and gathered in. As we shall also see, the differences at this point between title and encumbrance upon title become, or at least became, blurred for the English lawyer.

We have treated *nemo dat* as the working through of the logic of relativity of title in the context of the transfer of title. One can conclude by noting that its effects can be looked at from another point of view. *Nemo dat* can be seen as a principle which ensures the integrity and durability of an earlier title when the thing to which the title relates has passed into the hands of innocent later comers who know nothing of the earlier title. But its main significance is to highlight how fundamental to English law's conceptual scheme is the idea of relativity of title.

FRAGMENTATION OF TITLE: THE DIMENSION OF TIME

So far we have considered the relation between men and things principally from the point of view of space. But things, relations between men and things, and thus relations between men as mediated by things, can all be seen additionally from the perspective of time. Most obviously, things present themselves as a mechanism for transcending the inevitability of death, from the grandest mausoleum to the humblest grave.

Since death is something which will definitely happen, it is something people can, and do, make plans for in many societies, even if these plans are not formalised into a 'last will and testament' as in England. Of course, for the majority of people in England today, there is relatively little planning to do. Property transfers on death commonly take the form, so far as we can tell, of transfers of absolute interests across generations. When the parents die, the children sell the house and divide up the money between them. But death is not necessarily the only, or the most important, moment in the cycle of intergenerational transmission. A recent study by Musgrove and Middleton (1981) suggests that the most important transition for people from certain social groups is the entry into home ownership. The study finds that in these groups the transition is more decisive even than marriage. Among such groups, it is not uncommon for the parents of the new home owner to give him or her a cash sum which will meet some or all of the deposit. From a legal point of view this is simply a gift. But in fact it is probably one of the commonest forms of pre-mortem (for which see below) inheritance, where the second generation takes over property from the first generation before the latter's death.

A wide range of inheritance regimes is observable across cultures, even across Europe. The structure of any particular system of inheritance is largely shaped by the way in which it resolves two basic issues: the question of direction and the question of timing. In what direction – upon what categories of heirs – is the property to devolve? At what point or points in the developmental cycle of the family is property to be transmitted from one generation to another?

Every inheritance system is inevitably grounded in the attempt to organise intergenerational transmission of things, since such systems are attempts to organise the property consequences of human mortality. This is not to say that 'horizontal' systems are unknown: in some societies, things conventionally pass between elder brothers to younger brothers, as, in some instances, do thrones. This may especially be the case in polygamous cultures where brotherhood can span at least two generations, such that sibling succession can involve the succession to property – or power – by males who belong, in our terms, to the generation succeeding that of the brother from whom they inherit. In the most general terms, however, the proposition holds true: either things are destroyed on or before death, or some system must be developed for the passage across time through the generations of things which endure or are allowed to endure.

In England, as in the rest of Europe, the general direction of such transmission is 'vertical', and property devolves from parents to their children. So deeply rooted is this practice in Western culture that it needs to be stressed that this direction is not universal. Some African societies employ 'diagonal' systems. One example is a 'matrilineal' regime under which a man's property devolves upon his sister's son. Such systems inevitably throw up their own, subsidiary, questions: how is the relevant sister to be identified; and which of her sons is to take the property? As the anthropologist Lévi-Strauss emphasised, there are a limited number of possible elements, or forms that these questions can take, but a vast range of possible ways in which these basic elements can be combined.

In England, as we shall see, diagonal systems have been subordinated to vertical ones. Vertical devolution itself permits a further choice: on the one hand, all the property devolves upon a single heir, such that no division of the estate takes place ('impartible inheritance'); on the other, the patrimony is split up among or shared between several heirs, usually the children ('partible inheritance'). Impartible inheritance most commonly involves inheritance by the firstborn of the surviving males ('primogeniture'). Such a system poses the question of provision for the children who do not inherit. Must the heir maintain them, is alternative provision made for them, or must they make their own way in the world? We shall see in the next chapter that lawyers' attempts to accommodate these problems account for much of the complexity of English land law in the past, and, as a result, for its rather contorted contemporary shape.

Partible inheritance involves the alternative of shared, simultaneous enjoyment of the property or its actual division or subparcellization. Again, lawyers have had to accommodate this, and again we will see that it provides a further source of complexity. Finally, to anticipate what is discussed at length in the next chapter, two points should be noted. First, among different social groups,

both partible and impartible inheritance of land have long been practised in England, with the result that English lawyers have developed
mechanisms to give legal effect to the whole range of possible directions outlined above. Fragmentation of title in English law, which is
examined in the next chapter, is largely the result of attempts to
accommodate this diversity of inheritance systems. But, secondly,
we shall see that while the distinction between partible and
impartible inheritance accounts for the complex range of ways in
which lawyers conceptualise what in practical terms is co-ownership
of land within a family, the division between the two blurred in practice, which is why, as we shall also see, the distinction between fragmentation of title and incumbrances upon title is in certain cases
strained and awkward to maintain.

As we have said, the second crucial element of any system of
inheritance is timing, and, in particular, the way in which inheritance
and death are linked together or, for that matter, kept distinct. In
some systems, the death of a senior member of the family is the
moment at which his property passes to the next generation. In
others, devolution is channelled away from death, in one of two
ways. The most clear-cut method of such pre-mortem inheritance is
where devolution is completely detached from death so that most or
all of the senior member's property has already passed on to the next
generation when death occurs. In some societies, such a separation
of death from devolution is taken very seriously. Members of such
societies sometimes explain this by saying that devolution on death
encourages disputes between members of a family at the very
moment when the person best able to resolve them has gone. That is,
if succession always engenders disputes, pre-mortem inheritance has
the advantage of enabling elders who are 'out of the fray' to assist in
their resolution. Moreover, since where pre-mortem inheritance is
practised, devolution of property through generations tends to be a
drawn-out process phased over time in association with the important stages in the developmental cycle of the group – birth, puberty
and marriage as well as death – it avoids the potentially sharper or
more intractable conflicts over property which an abrupt, total transition might seem to generate. More generally, this type of
pre-mortem inheritance can be seen as a form of retirement on the
part of senior members, which is sometimes kept separate from with-
drawal from public or political life, as the indigenous observations

about the dispute settlement function of such elders outlined above indicate. In Western Christendom, this form of inheritance was sometimes stylised into a more elaborate renunciation of the world: the retiring elder divested himself of all his worldly goods and withdrew to a monastery to contemplate his soul. More practical reasons might induce a peasant farmer grown infirm through age to hand over his holding to the next generation; in such circumstances, he might make his maintenance a condition of the transfer (cf. Macfarlane, 1978: 136–8; 141–3). In twentieth-century England, pre-mortem inheritance has been the central mode of intergenerational transmission only for the rich, as the principal means of avoiding or limiting the inroads of the Inland Revenue upon private wealth.

The second main form of pre-mortem inheritance involves determining the direction of devolution before death but making death the relevant time for devolution to occur. As we see in the next chapter, the device invented by English lawyers which was known as the strict settlement, and which combined primogeniture with this intermediate form of pre-mortem inheritance, was one of the most important devices through which, by the seventeenth century, landownership passed through the generations, and it is no exaggeration to say that this has left a decisive mark upon English land law.

What we have discussed so far is not a set of legal rules, but rather the range of preferred inheritance patterns inscribed within particular cultures. Sometimes the English pattern was absorbed directly into English law, as in the rule, now abolished, that the heir at law (who was ascertainable through the principles of primogeniture) succeeded to the realty of a deceased who left no valid will. Legal systems vary in the degree to which they absorb and make mandatory certain inheritance practices. English law has long given pride of place to testamentary freedom, but as we have indicated above and develop in the next chapter, this does not mean that the norms which governed social practice encouraged people of property to take advantage of the freedom which the law allowed them.

What has been outlined so far is a set of preferred patterns stretching over time. They are preferred patterns in that they provide a grid of normative expectations, shape norms of proper conduct across generations, and provide a frame of reference for the resolution of disputes, whether or not the society in question has a specialised system of adjudication. But they are patterns of preference, encapsulating hopes and fears, a way of envisaging how the future should be but also a way of imagining bad futures, and thus, often again with the assistance of lawyers in some societies, a source of pressures to invent ways to make these bad, possible, outcomes at least bearable. If the systematisation of inheritance is rooted in the need to organise intergenerational transmission of property, it has to take account of the absence of preferred heirs, especially through infertility and infant mortality.

Where post-mortem inheritance is the norm, these possibilities at least permit straightforward, if painful, choices for the childless person about to die in a society where transmission in a vertical direction is the norm. As indicated above, the common alternative in such situations is diagonal inheritance, though this too can vary in the degree of precision which it assumes and the precise form in which it is inscribed as a desirable, second-best alternative. In Ancient Rome, for example, where infertility among the upper classes was not uncommon, adoption – usually though not necessarily of a blood relative – was one preferred solution in this situation (Hopkins, 1983: 49-50; 194-5). In England, this was not embraced, principally because the combination of an elaborate system of primogeniture and the intermediate form of pre-mortem inheritance which settled direction but not transmission before death was the dominant norm, and adoption in a full sense is most useful when you know that the possibility of a direct heir is no longer a practicable one. Roman adoption meant that your heir became, for all purposes, redesignated as if he was your direct heir; in England, with testamentary freedom, a pale imitation of this practice was followed in the face of infertility, whereby when property passed to a distant relative, he did not 'become' your son but you might dictate in your will that he adopted your surname as a condition of the property passing to him.

Where full-scale pre-mortem inheritance is practised, this question is also relatively manageable in the majority of cases. When the time comes for the elder to retire (however the 'rightness' of this time is arrived at) if he has no preferred successors, the property can be transferred to the second or third best, because the transmission occurs between living human beings. The accumulation of property in the Middle Ages by the Church of Rome is in part intelligible in this context. Someone retiring from the world preferred to give property to the Church rather than permit it to pass to distant relatives, who provided the only alternative destination (cf. Goody, 1983).

It is the intermediate system, the combination of determining the direction of property before death while retaining the event of death as the trigger for transmission, which presented the greatest structural difficulties. A will, of course, can be made years before death, and thus pose a problem of a similar kind. But in English law, a will can always be updated; if you make a new will, it revokes its precursors. However long before the death of its maker a will is made, it is not a form of pre-mortem inheritance in legal or social terms, because of this quality of revocabilty. Heirs made by will, in English law, are always heirs-expectant or apparent; not only can they lose everything if the will is revoked, but, in addition, if they die before the maker of the will, their rights lapse automatically. This is not exactly the case, as we see in the next chapter, with the intermediate form of pre-mortem inheritance which took the form of settlements of land. Here succession was made contingent upon the heir attaining his majority – conventionally, until 1969, the age of twenty-one for males, and now eighteen, and similarly for females unless they married below that age. Such a system threw up a simple problem which generated much legal complexity in order to accommodate it. When such a settlement was made – that is, when this type of pre-mortem inheritance was crystallised in legal, formal, terms – it would often be unclear who in the end would be the heir. This meant that such settlements had to provide for a range of possible alternatives, ranked in order of preference according to the normative framework within which members of the propertied classes, advised by their lawyers, worked. The legal complexities which this generated enable us to make some sense of the conceptual structure of English land law past and present; to this we now turn.

3

The Fragmentation of Title to Land

We must now outline the framework which English land lawyers created and within which they worked. We then look more closely at the goals which it came to be used to promote. We are now going to examine, in some detail, the ways in which English law permitted title to land to be fragmented. A later chapter considers how the principal problems from the point of view of the management of transfers of title to land were addressed and in large measure overcome in the 1925 legislation. Before tackling these matters, however, some clarification of a contextual kind is needed, without which some of the processes of fragmentation presented here may seem more mysterious than they were in reality.

A full overview of the legal framework of the ownership and enjoyment of land would, until recent times, require extensive discussion of the law of landlord and tenant as well as that concerning fragmentation of title. We have hived off most matters concerning landlord and tenant to other parts of this book, for the sake of convenience. But having said in earlier passages that lawyers have treated land as something special, it must now be said, with no less insistence, that 'land', and the legal arrangements for it, meant for many generations principally 'rents'. As we shall see, urban land ownership meant, in many cities – and still does in parts of some today – the ownership either of ground rents issuing from the land on which residential properties stood, or ownership of the houses or flats in question, which, as we shall also see, was leasehold, not freehold ownership. In the agrarian context, land ownership also meant ownership of a revenue-generating asset. A landed estate, large or small, commonly comprised a number of farms, each of which was normally rented out to tenants. This legal relationship too is considered below. All that needs emphasis now is that fragmentation of title meant, in sociological terms, the carving up of rental income, whether the source be ground rents, building rents or agricultural rents. What we are examining at this stage did not mean, in its essentials, the carving up of the use of land as such but of the revenue which it produced through time. Land is treated as special by lawyers; but what was really treated as special was land as a particular kind of source of revenue. Although we no longer, especially in the urban or residential context, talk in these terms, this is clearly expressed in the way in which economic historians talk about land prices in the past: they calculate their ups and downs, as people did at the time, in terms of so many 'years' purchase'. And what that means is that you calculate the capital value of land at any time with reference to the amount of annual income which it yields. Forty years' purchase means the price of land is high; twenty-five years' purchase means it is on the decline. Unless we keep firmly in mind that fragmentation of title meant fragmentation of rights to rental income, stretching over time, we will find land law and the reforms of 1925 unnecessarily mysterious and obscure.

There was an underside: someone had to pay these rents. The social and the economic histories of England until the twentieth century largely converge around, or could be written in terms of, this rent relation. The fact that from quite early times the rent relation assumed the form of payments of money is one fundamental reason why it is so difficult to pinpoint the 'moment' when England can usefully be said to have undergone the transition from 'feudalism' to 'capitalism'.

In the modern world, of course, the majority of people spend most of their lives paying rent for the house or flat where they live. But for us, this is principally an economic relation: the rent due to the council, the mortgage repayments due to the building society, weekly or monthly monetary outgoings not distinct from the quarterly electricity bill. In the past, by contrast, the rent relation was intertwined with a whole set of social relations of hierarchy and subordination. Rent bound people together socially and politically, as well as economically, in a fairly direct way. Today the relation is mediated by the central apparatus of government and its agencies, and is one element in general, 'macro' economic policy. In the past, it was largely constitutive of what society 'was'.

In the past, rent took many forms, and the conceptualisation of these differences was the province of lawyers. Rent divided society into two classes of people: those who owed something to another in the form of rent, and those to whom something was owed. The latter were the freeholders, the men and women who were free and therefore, in the case of the men, claimed the right to participate in the business of rule, if not, except in a few cases, in the affairs of state. Social function, economic status and political role are interconnected – interdependent – within this scheme of things. Only rights in common stood apart, in a certain way, from these representations of reality, for example, the right to pasture your sheep on common land. Rights in common were all but eliminated, over a long period of time, by a complex historical process, largely complete by the middle of the nineteenth century, whereby land was enclosed. As Yelling has emphasised, 'enclosure' covers three distinct processes. First, the 'laying together of scattered properties and consequent abolition of intermixture of properties and holdings'. Secondly, 'the abolition of common rights'. Thirdly, 'the hedging and ditching of the separate properties' whereby parcels of land, grouped together, are physically 'enclosed' (1977: 5).

Enclosure tended to sharpen the exclusive nature of the rent relation, partly because it eliminated common land, and partly because it destroyed some traditional forms of rent relations. And enclosure was an occasion for lawyers to come upon the scene because it involved the close scrutiny of occupiers' legal rights to the land that gave them their livelihood. In its earlier forms enclosure of land came about by 'agreement', sometimes approved by the Court of Chancery, and later it took place through Parliamentary processes. 'It was . . . an occasion when the legal title to common rights was closely scrutinised, and it is certain that throughout the country numerous claims for cottage common rights were rejected' (Yelling, 1977: 230).

Rent was central to the structure of the polity in matters of religion too. The Church of England was 'established' not just as an ideological system, but by means of the 'tithe', the share of rental income from land which was for a clergyman his living (for this see Evans, 1976). Enclosure had transformative effects here too, by 'commuting' the tithes and transforming them into the ownership of a defined parcel of land. Again, the variegated nature of the traditional rent relation was homogenised into one general form. This general form was what lawyers call the tenancy, and is examined below in Chapter 5.

For present purposes, three points need to be drawn out from the complex history of the rent relation. The first is that the imprint of the past upon the present has been most pronounced in terms of the schemes devised by lawyers to orchestrate over time the receipt of rents. This is the theme of the present chapter. The second point is that of the multitude of rent relations which existed in the past and to which lawyers directed their attention when necessary, the only survivor today of any importance, if we ignore mortgages, is the tenancy. Finally, the centrality of 'rent' in English society brings us to the core of what English lawyers mean by 'land'. It steers us, as it were, towards their metaphysics, to the ground of the way things are thought about rather than the way in which they can be said actually to exist.

In this chapter we examine the fragmentation of title to land from the point of view of what Marxists would call the exchange value of land. What is under scrutiny is a set of concepts which give expression to practices rooted in a particular view of how you calculate what land is worth, summed up in the catchphrase 'years' purchase'. Land is 'worth' a certain rental yield, and on the ground of that yield, the ingenuity of lawyers was principally deployed in inventing a range of mechanisms which could serve to guarantee, through potential enforcement by the courts and their coercive auxiliaries, the distribution of that yield in a range of ways which corresponded to the structure of social relations of English society in times past. We shall further see, in this and the next chapter, that it is difficult to draw a clear line between what is best regarded as a fragment of title from what is better called an incumbrance upon title. Both posed problems for the giving of good title; the legislative restructuring of 1925 was aimed at both.

We have inherited the concepts which derive from this past reality, in modified form, and these concepts now operate perhaps in a less directly expressive way, as the tools for legal conceptualisation of rather different social relations today. There is, in other words, a gap between the legal conceptualisation of social relations and lay sociological understanding of those relations in the modern world. In the past, the business of title, as we see in a later chapter, was hazardous, and this was why lawyers were needed to manage its transfer. In the modern world, partly but not wholly as a result of the 1925 legislation (it is also because what people want to do with land is, in legal terms, more simple), matters of title are less hazardous but more esoteric: in brief, land law is quite unintelligible to the layman of today, because its structures, embedded in the past, express next to nothing of his own experience of the world or of the way in which land mediates relations between people, or people and institutions. For these reasons, we have taken, throughout this work, 'history' to be the only way to embark upon understanding land law.

ESTATES IN LAND BEFORE 1926

Today, there are only two 'legal estates' which can exist in land: the 'fee simple absolute in possession' and the term of years absolute. When a house is advertised as freehold, it is the former estate in land which is offered, and when it is described as leasehold, it is the latter. Leases are examined in a later chapter. For the present, we can begin by noting that before 1926, the position regarding freehold estates in land was very different. There were three principal legal estates in land which could be created, each with its own distinctive character. The fee simple was the 'biggest' right – the whole interest in the land. But there were two lesser rights, the life estate and the fee tail or entail. The differences between the three relate to the possible duration of the interest created.

If X, the owner of land in fee simple, granted to A a life estate, A had a legal estate in that land for his lifetime. On his death, his estate came to an end because its duration had been limited to A's life. This meant that on A's death, he had no interest in the land which he could leave to his heirs, because his interest terminated on his death.

Equally, the *nemo dat* rule applied. If A sold his life estate to B, B acquired an estate which would come to an end on A's death, not on B's death, because the estate which A sold was limited by reference to the duration of A's life in the original grant. Lawyers said that in this situation B acquired an estate '*pur autre vie*' (that is, for the life of another (A)).

If X, the owner of land in fee simple, granted to A a fee tail, what happened? The entail was an estate whose duration was limited to the continued existence of a particular class of heirs. A grant of an entail was often expressed as follows: 'To A and the heirs of his body'. This created a succession of interests which would endure as long as the lineage founded by A. As long as there were descendants of A, the estate would continue, but if the position was reached when there was no one left alive who could trace his descent back to A, the estate came to an end. So if A only had one child, B, and B had three children, C, D and E, but all three died childless, the estate would end on the death of the last of the three. It did not survive through the descendants of A's collaterals, or through descendants of collaterals of A's ancestors.

If X, owner in fee simple, granted to A a fee simple, the position was different. Whereas the possible maximum duration of the entail is limited to the continued existence of a particular class of heirs, the possible maximum duration of the fee simple is not so limited, but can continue indefinitely until it comes into the hands of someone who himself has no heirs at all.

So, if A sells to B, the fee simple in the hands of B and his successors is not affected by the failure of A's lineage. And the same applies if B sells to C. A particular fee simple to land will only determine if the person into whose hands it has come dies without heirs. So, if C, who buys from B, dies (a) with no will and (b) with no living relatives who can succeed to his property under the intestacy rules, the estate comes to an end. Even if he died with no relatives, C could have 'made an heir' by making a will. It is the fact that he has died leaving no will and no relatives that determines the estate.

In each of the three examples, we have defined the nature of the respective estates in land with reference to the circumstances in which, at some date in the future, they may determine. This raised the question – what happens when they determine? Who then owns the land? In relation to the life estate and the entail, the answer is found by looking at an additional feature of the doctrine of estates, the distinction between present and future interests. In the case of the fee simple, the answer is found by considering the consequences of another doctrine, the doctrine of tenures, which provides the starting point for the role of Equity in land law and is thus outlined in the next chapter.

THE DOCTRINE OF ESTATES – PRESENT AND FUTURE INTERESTS

Since the fee simple is the 'biggest' right to land it follows that
- (i) if X grants A a life estate, or
- (ii) if X grants A a fee tail,

then in either case X has not divested himself of (parted with) his entire interest in the land. He has carved out of his greater estate a lesser estate. So when these lesser estates determine, X or his successors will get back the fee simple. But at the time of the grant, X is no longer entitled to present enjoyment of the land. He has a future interest, that is, a right to enjoyment at some time in the future, even though at the time of the grant it is not possible to say exactly when if ever the right to enjoyment will materialise.

When someone has a present right to enjoyment, lawyers say that the person has an estate or interest in possession. This does not mean that the person is in fact in possession of the property (because he may for example have leased it). It means that the person is entitled to present enjoyment of the land (one form of which is receiving rent from a tenant).

Where X has carved out a lesser estate from his fee simple, lawyers say that he retains a reversion in fee simple. This describes the fact that (a) he has parted with the present right of enjoyment, but (b) he has not parted with his entire bundle of rights in the land, because he has only created out of his fee simple a lesser estate. At some indeterminate date in the future, the lesser estates will determine, and then the reversion in fee simple will come into possession.

EXAMPLE If X, owner in fee simple, grants a life estate to A, A has a life estate in possession, X retains a reversion in fee simple. When A dies, X will have a fee simple in possession again. If during A's life, X sold his property rights – his reversion – to P, then, applying the *nemo dat* rule, P could be in no better position than X. When A died, P's fee simple would then fall into possession.

From this it follows that it was possible before 1926 to split the legal fee simple into a number of lesser estates, which could come into possession at different times. Thus in a grant it was possible not only to grant estates in possession, but also to create estates in the grant which would only take effect in the future. This enabled owners of property to create a whole series of successive interests in the same piece of land.

EXAMPLE X, owner in fee simple, grants to A a life estate. On A's death, B was to have a life estate. On B's death, C was to have an entail (i.e. an estate whose duration was limited to the continued existence of C's descendants). The future interests created here were called by lawyers remainders. So at the time of the grant:

A would have a life estate in possession;
B would have a life estate in remainder;
C would have an entail in remainder.

But even though X had carved out three interests from his fee simple, he still had not disposed of his whole bundle of rights because he never granted the fee simple to anyone. Therefore after C's entail, X has a reversion in fee simple.

On A's death:
(a) if B is still alive:
B has a life estate in possession;
C has a remainder in tail etc.;
(b) if B is dead (so that his life interest has already determined):
C has an entail in possession;
X has a reversion in fee simple.

In these examples, X could of course have created a remainder in favour of D to take effect when C's entail came to an end. If he had done that, then X would have granted away his entire interest in the land, and no reversion in his favour would arise on the grant.

The entail was a natural device for the lineage-oriented families of the medieval period, and the basic device of the perpetual entail was to be found throughout Western Europe, enduring largely unchanged in some countries until the era of codification (when it became one of codification's principal targets). In England, however, variations on this theme of tying the lineage to land and land to the lineage through the entail came to be played quite early, which centred upon the transferability of entails. We do not know exactly why and perhaps we never will. One reason might be that land-ownership in England was much more dispersed and fragmented than in many countries on the continent, and that this fact alone encouraged a more 'economic' orientation to landownership among the English landed classes than prevailed abroad. In any event, it is clear that lawyers were under pressure to find ways of making it possible for entailed estates to be bought and sold. Here we will simply note that the ways which were invented were exceedingly complicated, involving a cluster of fictitious formal transactions and fictitious court procedures. But it must be stressed that lawyers faced two distinct problems here.

The entail was principally a means of providing for the descent of rents through a lineage across time. It was not difficult for lawyers to invent mechanisms by which the person presently entitled to these rents could transfer his entitlement to a purchaser for the duration of his life. The difficulties were, first, could the claims of the heirs under the entail be barred, and, secondly, could ways be found for a purchaser from the present holder to acquire a title which was not put in jeopardy if the lineage to which the entail related failed? The first hurdle was the first to be overcome: fictitious mechanisms were invented which barred the claims of the lineage – and of the 'next in line' in particular – against the purchaser when the seller died. However, such a purchaser would only acquire a 'base fee', that is, a title which would terminate on the failure of the lineage, when there was no living person who could trace his descent directly to 'A and the heirs of his body'. By the late fifteenth century, this too was overcome, through more conveyancing ingenuity. This is sometimes attributed to the common law's inherent bias in favour of free alienability of land, but Simpson strikes a truer chord in suggesting that this bias '. . . is a grossly overworked explanation of oddities in medieval land law' and that 'it is much more likely that the judges were not so much influenced by views of policy, as by the difficulty of finding any technical flaws in a very ingenious device' (1961: 126). We are not concerned with the details of this device but only with its basic structure, which was put on a statutory footing in the Fines and Recoveries Act of 1833, and with the uses to which it was in fact put.

Once it became established that entails could be barred, one response might have been to try to defer its coming into effect by creating a string of successive life estates spanning several generations (to A for life, remainder to A's son for life, remainder to A's grandson for life etc.). Such an evasion of barrability was blocked by a number of common law rules, developed over a long period of time. These rules were of immense complexity, and many of them are now obselete. In broad terms, they were directed against the remoteness of vesting of absolute interests. The most important of the rules which survive today are known as the rules against perpetuities. These too are very convoluted, though they have been simplified somewhat for practical purposes by the Perpetuities and Accumulations Act 1964. All that can usefully be said, for present purposes, about this body of rules is that, in different ways and for different reasons, they restricted the range of unborn persons (like A's grandson where A is a child) in favour of whom interests in property could be created.

When an entail was barred, the owner in tail would from that time be able to deal with the land as if he was an owner in fee simple. Importantly, this meant that, after barring the entail, he could sell the land to a purchaser as an owner in fee simple. The effect of barring the entail was to shut out the remainderman or reversioner, destroying their rights. So if land was granted to A for life, remainder to B in tail, remainder to C in fee simple, B could bar the entail, thereby converting it into a fee simple, thus destroying C's rights.

At first, then, the device of barring the entail arose out of the search for mechanisms to alienate entailed estates. This in turn generated a new set of practices, which seem to have been fairly well defined by the late seventeenth century, which both made use of the device of barring the entail while, perhaps paradoxically, deploying the device so as to keep land in the family rather than alienate (sell) it. The practical effect, it was widely believed as late as the nineteenth century, was to tie up land over many generations within a particular lineage despite the barrability of entails. This was achieved by adopting a device known as the strict settlement, and land was kept within the family by a process known as settlement and resettlement.

What made all this possible was that the entail could only be barred by B:

(i) if the entail had come into possession, i.e., the life interests had determined, or

(ii) if the entail still being in remainder, B had the consent of the person with the prior estate.

This enabled land to stay in a particular family over many generations, although, as we shall shortly see when we examine it more closely, it did not guarantee such an outcome, however desirable that might have seemed to the people of the time.

At this point, the student coming to the subject for the first time is usually baffled, or convinced of the irrationality of the English law of property. How, the cry goes, could the law permit, in so blatant a way, the remainderman in fee to be robbed of what was his by right?

The device of the strict settlement was perfected by conveyancers towards the end of the seventeenth century. We explain its rationale in a moment; we must first outline its formal structure. The central structural features of this mechanism were as follows.

X grants land to A for life, remainder to B in tail, with remainders in fee simple over. (The remainders over – i.e., behind the entail – are not important, because A and B are going to bar the entail.) This grant of successive interests is called a settlement.

A and B agree to bar the entail. A's agreement is necessary because, as we have seen, B cannot bar the entail on his own because it is still in remainder. A and B therefore, acting together, now have control over the fee simple in the land. But the object of the exercise is to keep the land within the family. Therefore, having broken the settlement, they then proceed to resettle the land as follows: to A for life, remainder to B for life, remainder to B's eldest son in tail, with remainders over.

The settlement illustrates as well as anything the way English lawyers subordinate elegance or simplicity to the achievement of practical objectives. The strict settlement had one overriding objective, to ensure the passage of whatever estates were to be settled in such a manner as to maximize the possibility, from a legal point of view, that an identical passage could occur in the next generation.

Suppose you are a landed nobleman in your late fifties. Your eldest son and heir-presumptive (in English law, only God can make a heir) has just reached twenty-one (today, it would be eighteen) or, at perhaps a slightly older age, is about to marry. Suppose further that the principal family estates are already settled. You have a life estate in possession – you are what lawyers call the tenant for life. You draw the rental income from the estate. Next in line is your eldest son who has, at the moment, a remainder in tail. As always, there are remainders over, people further down the queue. We can leave over for the moment the question of who they are. If your son outlives you, he will, on your death, become a tenant in tail in possession and be able, as already seen, to bar the entail on his own and deal with the land on the basis that he is entitled in fee simple. You might feel sure that he would not, if that happened, rush off and sell or mortgage the ancestral estates; but your legal adviser would almost certainly tell you that it was best to leave nothing to chance. Much better for you and your son to get together, bar the entail while you are still around, and resettle the estates in such a way that the entail is pushed back a generation, with your son, under the new settlement, taking only a life estate in remainder which would fall into possession on the 'dropping' of your life.

Why should the son agree to the resettlement? No doubt, in the majority of cases, the question hardly arose: it was the done thing. And if the resettlement was to take place on the marriage of the son, the prospective wife's family might well insist upon it taking place as a condition of providing the dowry. Indeed, in the normal case of a settlement on marriage, the settlement would make specific provision for the dowry and who was to be entitled to what from it (on which more later). But apart from these factors, which probably explain why resettlement occurred in the majority of cases, there were ways in which parents could coerce their more recalcitrant heirs.

Because the resettlement could occur only when the son was of age, he would need cash in order to have fun in town. How could he raise the money otherwise? He and his father came to an arrangement whereby if the son agreed to the resettlement, an income would be raised for the son out of the estate. The only other way the son could raise money would be by mortgaging or selling his entail, but that would be like selling his inheritance for a bowl of soup, and would cause a scandal in society. Some did; the balance of advantage for most lay in acquiescing in the wishes of their parents.

This pattern could be, and often was, repeated every generation. When A died, after the resettlement, his son would have only a life estate in possession, and A's grandson would now have the entail in remainder. When the grandson reached his majority, the same thing would happen all over again.

The central object of this settlement–resettlement device, then, was to prevent the entail from ever coming into possession. Once that happened, the tenant in tail could bar the entail as we have seen. That would mean that he now had a fee simple, and would be able to alienate (sell) the land away from the family. But we still have not penetrated the mystery of why the law colluded in shutting out the 'claims' of the remaindermen behind the entail being barred. We can see the practical logic underpinning this now if we look more closely at a typical settlement.

Suppose the new settlement, made on the heir-presumptive's marriage, looks something like this.

1. To A for life. A is the head of the family and under the new settlement remains entitled, by virtue of the life estate in possession, to the rental income from the family estates.
2. To B (the heir-presumptive) for life.
3. Then to the first son of B on the body of B's first wife and the heirs male of the body of such first son lawfully to be begotten (i.e. excluding bastards).
4. Then to the second son of B on the body of B's first wife and the heirs male of his body etc.
5. Then to the third son etc. down to the tenth son of B.

If the settlement stopped here, it would fail to provide for the devolution of the estates in the event of the marriage which occasioned the settlement in our example producing no male children who survived. And the whole point of the exercise was to think about such possibilities in advance. Two principal choices presented themselves in the event of a failure in the 'direct' male line. Either the estates could pass on to the daughters or, as readers of *Pride and Prejudice* should recall, they could move collaterally, following the same pattern, to the junior male line. To simplify, if B had one brother, C, at the time of the settlement, and succession through males was the preferred family choice, we would have:

6. To B's brother C for life.
7. Then to C's first son and the heirs male of his body etc. down to C's tenth son lawfully begotten etc.

In such cases, only then would we find:

8. To the daughter or daughters of B.

The order could of course be reversed, with B's daughter or daughters taking in preference to the male heirs of the younger son. And, further, female succession could be organised in a number of ways. Daughters could take in order of seniority or in equal shares. If the former, it would be essential to spell out what should happen if a daughter died without issue. If, as was probably usual, she took in tail male, the estate would pass to a collateral male on her death.

For the sake of completeness, there will be a remainder in fee simple in the settlement. But this remainder was, for all concerned, something remote. The classical settlement meant that someone would, short of genealogical catastrophe, inherit the estates long before the ultimate remainderman was reached, preferably as a tenant for life (inheritance by the next generation); more risky, especially from a legal point of view, succession by a tenant in tail from the second generation (viz, one of A's male grandchildren); failing that, succession by the women of the family. The strict settlement belongs to a world now far away. But it is hard to exaggerate its centrality if one wants to understand the 'close texture', in Maitland's phrase, of English land law, or the organising categories of our modern, statutory, system of land law and conveyancing.

Many of those involved in the teaching of property law would acknowledge the way in which the sense of the past is deeply imprinted upon the fabric of the present corpus of doctrine, which constitutes in the last instance the pedagogical *raison d'être*. The strict settlement of the past contours perhaps more than any other legal device the present landscape of our law.

The discussion so far has centred around the structural consequences for English land law of the practice of impartible inheritance – and of primogeniture in particular – among certain strata of the English landed classes in the past. This has left open the question of what provision was made for people other than the emergent heir, like the widow of the tenant for life and the younger brothers and sisters of his successor. An examination of this dimension of the strict settlement reveals further sources of complexity, and should help us to understand better the rationale which underpinned the precise shape of the framework adopted in 1925.

Provision in strict settlements for wives and anticipated dependent children could be secured in a number of ways. For children, the most flexible device was to convey a lease to trustees on trust to 'raise portions', but it was often the case that this device, or a rent charge, was attached to some of the family estates only, and the 'main' estates, with which the family was most closely associated (which, again, might mean those which had descended through the male line rather than come to the family through marriage) might be kept free of such charges. The aim was to provide a capital sum for use as a dowry by the daughters and a provision by the younger sons, though these capital sums might not be paid over for many years, and the sons and daughters receive only interest on the capital, which, in legal terms, belonged to them.

Much no doubt was left to private negotiation and family consensus, when the portions were due but the capital unavailable. Unmarried daughters may have been especially vulnerable to postponement of the capital sum in the interests of the family at large, at various times hedged in by agricultural depressions and galloping charges. The formal legal rights must often have constituted merely a backdrop against which this informal negotiation and 'compromise' occurred. An unmarried daughter might thus defer calling for her portion, and instead remain effectively dependant on receiving interest payments from her family. For a daughter who married, her portion, whether realisable on marriage, or, through interfamilial negotiation, only later, in some sense represented the basis for calculating her 'jointure', the provision for her widowhood.

What is significant about the strict settlement is the temporary nature of the property provision, a provision for widowhood only, after which the estate of the husband's family would be discharged of a liability. The jointress of such a dynastic settlement generally had very little formal 'say' in the transmission of property to the next generation, unless, as seems rare, significant property had been settled upon her, at the time of or after her marriage, to her separate use. This seems from the available evidence to have been relatively uncommon in the case of dynastic families, who sought to provide for so many contingencies at the time the strict settlement was made.

It might then not be too farfetched to suggest that women who belonged to or married into dynastic families were marginal in terms of the control which they had over the family property. This point is highlighted not only by the absence of control over intergenerational transmission, but by the very nature of the jointure, which effectively, in its developed form, left the widow in the position of a mere passive recipient of an income secured upon some or all of the family estates, with no formal control over the management of the property (though she could obstruct a sale).

The jointure can be compared with the medieval modes of provision for widows, which survived in some agricultural communities until at least the eighteenth century. Under the medieval common law, a widow had a right of dower over all the freehold estates of which her husband had been seized at any time during the marriage, even if he had alienated them before his death. Under the common law, she had a right to a third of the rents and profits from the land during her widowhood at the expense of the husband's heir. The husband had a similar right over his wife's estates, called a tenancy by courtesy. 'Freebench', the equivalent provision where the land was held by customary tenure, variously gave the widow a third or a half of the rents and profits, according to the custom of the manor. For the propertied classes, such an automatic, status-based means of securing provision came to be regarded as inconvenient quite early. They interfered with any form of planning. The jointure was evolved as a device for planning the provision; what is significant is the transformation in the nature of the jointure itself, in its increasing subordination to primogeniture and intergenerational transmission.

Originally, in Tudor times, jointure involved conveying certain lands to husband and wife as joint tenants (see further below). On the death of one spouse, the survivor would be exclusively entitled to the rents and profits, and would further be exercising powers of control and management over this portion of the family estates. 'Joint tenancy' was the origin of jointure, but denoted a more active, more participatory role for a woman during widowhood. It denotes a form of planning, but not necessarily intergenerational planning. If made by way of dower, it would exclude the common law rights. Elaborate devices were conceived by conveyancers to exclude dower, culminating in the Dower Act 1833. But during the same period, jointure was attenuated to a mere right to receive a certain revenue, and open to criticism at that for burdening the rent rolls at the expense of agricultural improvement.

In the dynastic settlement, where in the nature of things much thought was likely to be given to the devolution of the property in the event of a failure in the direct male line, more variation occurred, as we have already seen. Christopher Clay (1968) has demonstrated a number of these, in the course of casting doubt upon the centrality of marriage and settlement in the rise of great estates in the eighteenth century. Writing in the nineteenth century, Sugden advised that in the event of failure in the direct male line, there should be partible inheritance by the daughters, rather than succession in tail male in order of seniority, because of the inconvenience of the estate passing backwards and forwards from one branch of the family to another if collateral male descent was consistently followed. (1858: 113) Clay has suggested that in the eighteenth century, a failure of direct males was often followed by the paterfamilias making an increased, perhaps 'extravagant' provision for the daughters. This could well have endured into the nineteenth, though the Victorian enthusiasm for agricultural improvement may have tempered such practices.

The dynastic ambition which fuelled the strict settlement was not, as indicated above, universal among the landowning classes of England in past times. Lawyers had to accommodate pressures from urban elites in particular and to some extent from those with more modest agricultural holdings which pushed further in the direction of partible inheritance. By its very nature, partible inheritance always poses a basic choice between actual division of the inheritance – what lawyers came to call 'partition' – and concurrent enjoyment by the inheritors of the patrimony. This second possibility was stylised by lawyers into something called the 'tenancy in common'. Tenants in common had 'undivided shares' in land. No such co-owner could point to a particular room in a house or a field in a farm and call it their own. Rather, he or she shared generally with the other co-owners in the enjoyment of the land. This is not mysterious if we remember that 'enjoyment' was primarily geared to the receipt of rents, and the tenancy in common was thus a mechanism for sharing out a rental income among members of a family over time directly, rather than indirectly through the more contorted mechanisms of the dynastic settlement discussed above, in which, in legal terms, the income from the estate 'belonged' to the tenant for life, but was overlaid with a multiplicity of claims from the widows, daughters and younger sons.

The Fragmentation of Title to Land

The tenancy in common stood in contrast to another form of co-ownership called the joint tenancy. The difference is tied up with the consequences of the death of a co-owner. Someone who died a joint tenant had nothing which could pass, through will or intestacy, to his or her heirs. The 'share' of such a person in the enjoyment of the land simply added to that of the surviving joint tenants. In other words, if there were three joint tenants, each would be entitled while they lived to a third each of the income arising from the land. If one of them died, the survivors would take one half of the rents each. By contrast, the death of a tenant in common would lead to his own entitlement passing on to his heirs. And insofar as it involved a share in a rental income, it could over time become extensively fragmented, with the consequence that, in due course, as we shall see, transfer of a title held in common in this way could become an extremely complex affair.

So far, we have presented fragmentation of title as principally a consequence of the circulation of land through time, of lawyers' attempts to accommodate a diverse range of strategies geared to pre- and post-mortem inheritance. As long as people settled their land in the way described above, conveyancing was a slow process and land hard to sell, because the life estate and the entail were unattractive commercial propositions for purchasers. The 1925 legislation, therefore, attempted to facilitate the conveyancing process itself, and to make all or most land sellable. It achieved these two related objectives by making it impossible after 1925 to split the fee simple into successive lesser legal estates. This was brought about by saying that, after 1925, the entail and the life estate could only exist in equity, and a modified terminology was adopted to reflect this change. The language of 'estates' was abandoned, and today we speak of 'entailed interests' and 'life interests'. Because they can only exist today in equity, they can only exist behind some form of trust. We must now consider what it means to speak of 'trusts' and 'equitable interests'.

4

Equity

'Equity' has had a long innings in the history of philosophy. What
exactly it meant or means today as a philosophical theme is as elusive
as the attempt to say what 'justice' means. One aspect of the difficulty is the same in each case: each idea has something to do with the
way in which we think about what law is, or claims to be or to provide. In each case too, it is generally recognised that no actual legal
system can provide perfect equity or perfect justice. Perhaps Kant is
the most blunt when he calls equity 'a silent goddess who cannot be
heard' (1797; tr. 1965: 40).

The other way of embarking upon the study of equity is to follow
the example of an historian such as Maitland, who saw equity as a
body of doctrines, rules and practices which has arisen out of the
work of a distinct set of courts. These courts did not spring up fully
armed at some moment in time. They did not emerge as the result of
some plan, but gradually over time as English monarchs reacted to
the demands placed upon them. So intimate was the connection
between monarch and the principal court which emerged – the
Court of Chancery – that during the interregnum many sought,
unsuccessfully, its abolition. The weakening of this intimate
link between monarch and chancery was a precondition for equity
to 'settle down' and become a set of rules administered by a set
of courts more or less like any other, albeit with a distinctive
character.

The King's Courts of the Middle Ages (King's Bench, Common
Pleas, Exchequer, and the Assize Courts) were particularly concerned with resolving disputes which today we would describe as
involving the criminal law, land law and tort. Access to these courts
depended principally upon obtaining the appropriate 'Writ' from
the King's Chancellor, that is, from the Keeper of his Great Seal, the

fixing of which to a document impressed it with the royal authority. To seek redress for any wrong in the courts, a complainant had to bring his case within one of the writs available. Over time, this system became increasingly elaborate, and a central concern of the royal courts became whether the pleadings (the plaintiff's statement of the wrong complained of in the writ) were correct in every detail. If some mistake had been made in the pleadings, the plaintiff would often be denied his remedy. This led to dissatisfaction among litigants, and an increasing volume of petitions began to come before the King requesting that he should give redress and do justice where his courts had not done so.

One particular way in which the common law courts of the Middle Ages failed to respond to the demands placed upon them concerns us here. This is what became known as the 'use'. In order to understand this, we must consider briefly one of the cornerstones of medieval land law, the doctrine of tenures. Leaving aside his claim to be entitled by right of blood, William the Conqueror held England from 1066 by right of conquest. He acquired the kingdom of England, he did not inherit it, as he did his duchy of Normandy. (This may be why the kingdom devolved on his death to his second son, and the duchy to his eldest.) As a result, all land in England was 'held', directly or indirectly, of the King. The 'doctrine of tenures' was the elaboration by medieval lawyers of the range of conditions upon which land was so held. At various times from 1066 onwards, this land had been granted to barons, who held as tenants of the Crown. All grants were conditional – that is, land was granted in return for certain kinds of services. These might involve the provision of knights (knight tenure) or agricultural produce (socage), etc. We will concentrate on knight tenure here. Someone who held land of the King in knight tenure might himself grant some of that land to others. In early feudalism, this would usually be done by subinfeudating, that is, by the tenant creating his own tenant and becoming himself a lord as well as a tenant of the Crown. And this second grant would also be conditional, and might well in this example have been itself a grant in knight tenure.

This process could continue, with a whole chain of lords and tenants, each tenant, within such a hierarchy, owing loyalty expressed through homage and the provision of services to his immediate lord, each lord, in return, owing protection to his subordinate. The history of this system, royal efforts to stop subinfeudation, the later disintegration into what is sometimes called 'bastard' feudalism, even the adequacy of the term 'feudalism' itself for understanding the character of medieval social and political relations, need not concern us here.[5] The military tenures, which we use here for illustrative purposes, were abolished in 1660. Most vestigial remains of the doctrine were removed by 1925, but still today all land is held by virtue of this doctrine of the Crown.

As we have seen, tenurial relationships meant that most people holding land owed services to their immediate lord. These services became less significant over time, especially in relation to military tenures. This was because they began to be commuted to fixed money rents. Instead of providing a knight, the tenant just paid a fixed sum of money. With inflation in the late Middle Ages, these fixed payments became less significant.

But, in addition, lords had other important rights over the land of their tenants. These were known as the 'incidents' of feudal tenure. If a knight tenant died, his heir had to pay to the lord a relief before he could enter into his inheritance. If on the death of his father, the son was still a minor, the lord had a right of wardship, which meant that the lord could take whatever produce or rent the land yielded until the son came of age. These rights were inflation-proof, and so became of great value to lords, and especially to the Crown, as the value of the services declined. Not unnaturally, wardship was resented, and people began to seek ways of minimizing its effects.

Military tenures were connected, both in their origin and their supposed function, with fighting. Suppose, then, that such a tenant went off to war, from a sense of duty either to his King or to his God, or in the hope of booty, not knowing if and when he would return. What provision could he make for his family during his absence? One scheme was to transfer his legal estate to a relative or friend who was staying behind, who could look after it and administer it until he returned, or who, should the knight die abroad, could take care of it until the knight's son reached his majority and could take it over himself.

So the tenant transferred his estate but did not intend to allow the grantee to benefit from the land personally. Rather, he was to look after it on behalf of the grantor's family. The grantee was morally a custodian of the land, and not entitled to use it for his own purposes.

But if the grantor died in the Crusades, was there any way in which his family could prevent the grantee from taking the benefit for himself? If they went to the common law courts, they would be told that the legal estate in the land was vested in the grantee, and that he was entitled to the benefit himself. The family was not recognised by the common law as having any rights in the land.

So the family might petition the King, arguing that although the strict legal rights in the land were vested in the grantee, nevertheless, his conscience was bound by the circumstances in which he had acquired that estate. It was wrong for the grantee to be able to assert his legal rights against the family.

These appeals to the King came to be delegated to his Chancellor, the keeper of the King's conscience as well as his seal. The Chancellor was usually a man of the church. Around him grew up what became an early form of 'bureaucracy' – the Chancery. Appeals against the injustices of the common law came to be taken to the Chancery, and the basis of its jurisdiction to 'mitigate the rigour of the common law' was its origin in medieval notions of conscience.

When petitions from such families found their way into the Chancery with some frequency, the Chancellor came to recognise that the conscience of the grantee was bound. His authority proceeded against the person, i.e. the Chancellor would forbid the grantee to take the benefit himself, under threat of imprisonment. By doing this, the Chancellor was beginning to recognise the rights of the family against the grantee as something more than personal. They were beginning to have property rights of some kind, because by preventing the grantee from asserting his legal rights to enjoyment of the land, the Chancellor was in effect saying that those rights belonged to the family. And so in the course of time, we come to speak of these rights as equitable rights (because they have their origin in the protection of Equity or the Court of Chancery) or equally we refer to them as 'beneficial rights' because they tell you not who has the legal title (the legal estate) but who is entitled to enjoyment or the benefit of the land. In other words, these early inventions by the Chancellor marked the beginning of what is today a commonplace of English jurisprudence – the splitting of rights of ownership into legal rights (title) and equitable rights (the right to enjoyment).

This device, of granting land to X for the benefit of Y, became known as the 'use'. X held the title 'to the use of' Y. Whatever its origins, it became used in the late Middle Ages as a way of circumventing the problems caused by the incidents of feudalism.

As explained above, these became due on the death of the tenant. So, if someone was old or thought he was about to die, and his heir was a young boy, the dreadful prospect of a long wardship looked inevitable. But the use provided a way of avoiding the incidents. The tenant could grant his estate to a much younger man 'to uses' (for the benefit of his heir). If he did this, then when he died, the incidents would not arise, because he had not died as a tenant, and the incidents only arose on the death of someone who died as a tenant of his lord. When the heir was of age, the grantee could then transfer the estate to him, having administered the land in the meantime for the benefit of the family, and the arduous wardship would have been avoided.

In Tudor times the Crown became particularly concerned about the loss of revenue which resulted from resort to such uses, and in 1536 Henry VIII forced through a reluctant Parliament the Statute of Uses which abolished many of the uses discussed above. Popular discontent at this Statute led Henry to give ground four years later, and allow uses of a part of a man's land to be created in a will (Statute of Wills, 1540).[6]

The effect of the Statute of Uses was that for several years uses ceased, with limited exceptions, to be recognised if created *inter vivos*. But in the late seventeenth century, the use effectively reappeared in what has become its contemporary form, the 'trust'. Like the use, the trust permits obligations to be attached to property of any kind, requiring it to be applied in a particular way, and such obligations are enforceable in a court of equity. Trusts of property were not confined to trusts of land, even if, as we have seen, its precursor, the use, did originate in the context of land and the tenurial relationships of the Middle Ages. Much of the 'learning' of the law of trusts, indeed, is concerned with trusts of funds rather than with trusts of land. Because, however, we are concerned here with trusts of land, our central focus is upon the more limited notion of the trust as involving a splitting of ownership rather than upon the more diffuse idea of the trust as a form of equitable obligation attached to property. And it must suffice for the moment to note that while English law permitted the fragmentation of the fee simple 'at law' into life estates and entails, the importance of trusts of land was less than it now is.

As outlined above, one linchpin of the 1925 reforms was the abolition of the life estate and entail as legal estates in land. The reasons for this were embedded in the difficulties which such fragmentation generated for the management of the process of land transfer by lawyers, which is why the details of these reforms are considered in later chapters of this book. For the moment, what matters is that the life estate and entail were not abolished as such: the strategy of reform proceeded on the basis that the substance of these devices should be preserved, but that, for conveyancing reasons, they could only 'subsist' behind a trust.

In simple terms, the 1925 legislation made trusts of land much more important, and 'equity' much more significant in terms of the manner in which disputes in the courts arising out of the ownership and occupation of land could be framed. Many more questions to do with the enjoyment of land now rest within the province of equity than was the case in the past. Ownership of the fee simple has been reduced, conceptually, to a matter of the ability to give good title, to the capacity to engage in exchange. Use rights which approximate to the incidents of ownership are issues for equity: an absolute owner of land is now called the sole beneficial owner, the term 'beneficial' indicating the interposition of equity in conceptualising rights. As we shall see in the next chapter, this leads to some curious reversals, at the conceptual level, in lawyers' traditional ordering of priorities. Lesser use rights, like easements, were permitted in 1925 to continue to function as legal interests, and a leasehold interest in land remained, along with the fee simple, the only legal estate capable of existing in land after 1925. There is no underlying logic to this scheme of things. It is intelligible only in terms of practical convenience, and in terms of how, given such a legislative framework, it is possible to frame a dispute or pose a question in the courtroom. The conceptual scheme of English land law is as it is for practical reasons; in no way is it sensibly regarded as the product of 'Reason' in some larger sense. In this way, the 'artificial' character of English law, as opposed to the 'natural' reason of the civilian lawyer, which continental codification was meant to embody, persists through the ambitious English 'codification' of 1925.

The development of the 'rules' of Equity was dependent upon the gradual transformation of the royal secretariat into part of the judicial apparatus of England. At first, the Chancellor intervened on an ad hoc, case-by-case basis, deciding petitions in terms of what conscience required. There was, at this stage, no clear sense of the application of rules and therefore no significant conception of precedent or rule-following. 'Rules' began to emerge insofar as typical fact-situations came to be seen as being appropriate occasions for the intervention of equity and the granting of an equitable remedy. But until the conflicts between King and Parliament which led to the Civil War and the execution of the King in 1649, no clear boundaries or limits were recognised by the Chancery to its jurisdiction. This became especially pronounced during the reign of James I (1603–25). It led to a collision between equity and the common law courts over the limits of the equitable jurisdiction. Problems arose for example over equity's use of a remedy known as the 'injunction'. Equity might forbid someone from bringing an action in the common law courts. Could it also forbid a successful plaintiff in the common law courts from enforcing his judgement against a defendant who had petitioned the Chancery to intervene? In this conflict, equity justified its activity in the same way as James I explained his notion of kingship in relation to Parliament and the common law. James argued that God's Law was above secular or 'ordinary' law (i.e. the common law). It was the King who 'knew' God's Law because the King's conscience was a faculty bestowed by God enabling him to discern God's law. For James, indeed, Kings were Gods (Oakley, 1984: 93ff). The absolute power of kings could not be discussed by their subjects, just as it was blasphemy to discuss whether there were limits upon God's omnipotence. The Chancellor was the Keeper of the King's conscience. When the conflict between the common lawyers led by Sir Edward Coke CJ, and the Chancery under Lord Ellesmere came to a head, James consequently resolved the problem in favour of the Chancery. This is how Ellesmere explained the decision of the King. 'The Chancellor sits in Chancery according to an absolute and uncontrollable Power, and is to judge according to that which is alleged and proved; but the judges of the common law are to judge according to strict and ordinary (or limited) powers.'[7]

Thus, during this period leading up to the Civil War, the position of equity was very much tied up with the position of the King within the polity. While this was later transformed, James's decision is carried through to the modern law in the maxim 'Equity prevails over law'.

We cannot elaborate here upon what this notion of 'absolute' power meant to political theorists of the time. It must suffice to observe that this way of thinking about royal power had a long ancestry and was a centrepiece of medieval ideas about the nature of government. It was only minimally connected with the idea of 'absolute' royal power which came to prominence in France much later in the seventeenth century, was visualised in the construction of Versailles, and was carried through to its logical conclusion in Prussia and later in Austria-Hungary in the eighteenth century. How and to what extent English governmental arrangements changed during this period are matters of considerable dispute. Quite undue prominence has been given to the writings on government of John Locke and to the ideology of the social contract (see Clark, 1985 and 1986). But for our purposes the most significant change was perhaps the incorporation of the court of Chancery into the regular judicial apparatus of the polity, and thus the removal of the monarch from any direct input into the judicial process (apart from the retention of the prerogative of mercy). Thus Lord Nottingham, Lord Chancellor after the Restoration, said that the conscience which should guide the Chancellor was not '*naturalis et interna*' but '*civilis et politica*'. What this meant was quite simply that the Chancery had become a court like any other, part of the 'ordinary' power of government – i.e. subject to law – and not part of the absolute, uncontrollable, undiscussable power of the sovereign. And in 1734, Jekyll, MR, described the basis of equitable remedies as being '*secundum discretionem boni viri*', a '*bonus vir*' being someone '*qui consulta patrum, qui leges juraque servat*'. (Equity was to be dispensed 'according to the judgement of a man of virtue', such a man being one who 'upheld the decrees of Parliament and the law'.)

One anomaly did remain, though it perhaps seemed less odd in the past than it does today. As long as the Chancellor presided over Chancery – which he continued to do until the Judicature Acts of the 1870s – his office uniquely contradicted whatever tenuous version of the separation of powers emerged in eighteenth-century political theory in England. He was an officer of state, and when the 'cabinet' system developed, he was – and remains – a member of the executive. He was, and is, a member of the legislature because he was and is a peer of the realm. That this was tolerated tells us something about how people of the time understood the character of the 'merely civil' law, the work of the Chancery in supervising the administration of trusts, settlements and wills. It was part of the business of government but not, in our terms, part of the political process or that part of the judicial process which bore upon the liberties of the subject. The idea of the Lord Chief Justice sitting in the cabinet was, by contrast, much more controversial and a very rare occurrence. Such an arrangement was not illegal or unconstitutional, but many thought it inexpedient 'because it tended to excite a suspicion of political partiality in the administration of justice'. 'It would not be proper', said Lord Eldon in the House of Lords, 'that the same individual should act, first as a minister to institute prosecutions for treason and sedition, and afterwards as the judge to preside at the trials' (Twiss, 1846: 352).

The origins and subsequent history of equity can be said to lie in the nature of the remedial assistance it came to afford. The systematised form of this assistance must serve as our point of departure.

The two principal remedies are specific performance and the injunction. Both reflect the once intimate association of Chancery with the absolute power of the King. A decree of specific performance is an order by the court requiring someone to do something (i.e. to perform a contract), and the injunction is an order by the court forbidding someone to do something. Both issue against the person (they are called remedies *in personam*). Today this means that if the person against whom they are issued disobeys the order, he will be in contempt of court and may face imprisonment. Both remedies can be seen as the marshalling of the power of what today we call the British state behind 'private' transactions concluded by people with the help of their lawyers. As we shall see, from the perspective of courts rather than conveyancers, the role of specific performance of the contract for the sale of land was pivotal for the way in which the courts formulated over time the 'principles' of English land law.

Both remedies are discretionary. This means that they are not available as of right. By contrast, common law remedies, notably damages, are available as of right once the plaintiff has proved his case (e.g. that a contract has been breached by the defendant). The only discretion or flexibility which the court possesses in an award of common law damages is in fixing the quantum of those damages. This discretionary quality of equitable remedies means that in certain circumstances the plaintiff will be denied his equitable remedy even though he has proved a wrong against him which is normally remedied by equity.

There are four main circumstances where the equitable remedy will be denied. First, where damages at law would provide adequate compensation for the wrong suffered. Secondly, where the plaintiff's own conduct is reproachable ('He who comes to Equity must come with clean hands'). Thirdly, where, because of what has happened, it is impossible or impracticable to award the equitable remedy. Sometimes, for example, because third parties are involved, awarding specific performance of a contract would only lead to further litigation. In these circumstances, where the plaintiff would normally have been given his decree of specific performance but for the complication of third parties, the courts have jurisdiction to award equitable damages in lieu of specific performance. Although the plaintiff will only receive financial compensation instead of the promised performance, an award of equitable damages can lead to the award of a significantly greater quantum of damages. This is because the quantum is assessed on the loss as it stands at the time of the trial of the action, rather than on the loss at the time of the breach of the contract (which is the basis for assessing contractual damages at common law). Finally, the remedy is normally denied where the person asking for the remedy of specific performance is a volunteer, that is, has not given consideration.

In the mature period of equity, when its courts had come to be integrated into the ordinary judicial apparatus of the English polity, its jurisdiction was described by lawyers as threefold: the exclusive, the concurrent and the auxiliary jurisdiction.

The exclusive jurisdiction involved the enforcement of equitable rights; the concurrent jurisdiction involved the enforcement of legal rights. This jurisdiction was exercised 'either because the remedy in equity was a more perfect remedy than the remedy at law, or because the remedy at law either never existed at all, or [had] become unavailable' (Snell, 1908: 424). The auxiliary jurisdiction 'was applicable primarily to the better enforcement of legal rights, – and only (by a sort of analogy) was it applicable to the enforcement also of equitable rights . . . (in the case of legal rights) the decision of the common law court thereon was conclusive in equity; but . . . (in the case of equitable rights) the opinion of the common law court (where equity thought fit to take that opinion) was for guidance only, – and the verdict also of a common law jury (where equity thought fit to obtain such verdict) was for guidance only' (ibid.: 603). All matters relating to trusts, mortgages, married women and lunatics were part of the exclusive jurisdiction; specific performance and the injunction were at the core of the concurrent jurisdiction; orders for discovery and delivery of documents, were, for our purposes, a central element in the auxiliary jurisdiction.

In former times, litigants sought the assistance of equity where their rights derived from the common law, partly because of the remedies which equity courts made available, and, in some cases at least, because of the absence of a jury (which was once commonplace in civil actions). A case from 1735 provides a good example.[8] A Duke owned an antique altarpiece, which had been taken and sold to a goldsmith who knew of the Duke's claim. The Duke presented a bill in equity for delivery of the thing. The goldsmith said the court should leave the plaintiff to his remedies at law. Delivery of title-deeds ('writing savouring of the realty') and heirlooms, he conceded, might be appropriate things for equitable assistance, but if bills like this were allowed, he argued, the equity courts would be swamped with petitions concerning the wrongful taking or retention of things which had previously been tried in the courts of common law, a kind of argument, of course, which is as old as the hills.

The Lord Chancellor helped the Duke out. With things of 'curiosity or antiquity', he thought, it would be hard if plaintiffs could only recover their value; that would be like a forced sale. A later judge supplies a further clue. The Duke had brought his bill before the Lord High Chancellor of England; but pursuit of things of curiosity and antiquity through the common law courts might have proved to be quite a different affair. The common law required the thing to be found, and most moveables could be hidden. It was thus much more likely, going down that road, that a plaintiff would end up only with financial compensation, and the amount would fall to be determined by a jury.

> The Pusey horn, the patera of the Duke of Somerset, were things of that sort of value that a jury might not give twopence beyond the weight. It was not to be cast to the estimation of people who have not those feelings. In all cases where the object of the suit is not liable to a compensation by damages, it would be strange if the law of this country did not afford any remedy. It would be great injustice if an individual cannot have his property without being liable to the estimate of people who have not his feelings upon it.[9]

To invoke the assistance of a court of equity, it was insufficient to make good your claim at law. Unless you could assert an 'equity' (i.e. something that warranted an appeal to equity, preferably, of course, grounded in the established practice of that court), you would be left to your remedies at law, such as they were.

In the 1870s, significant procedural and administrative changes were made which enabled the rules of equity and the rules of common law to be discussed in the same court before the same judge. These changes culminated in the abolition by the Judicature Acts of the existing common law courts and the Court of Chancery, and their replacement by a single unified High Court of Justice, divided up into three main divisions, Queen's Bench, Probate, Divorce and Admiralty (now Family), and Chancery.

Lawyers still debate the precise consequences of the Judicature Acts. What is clear is that they brought about a change in procedure, such that both equitable and common law remedies are now available in the same court. Before these Acts, many litigated issues to do with property and title belonged excusively to the courts of common law. Equity was resorted to in order to supplement the jurisdiction of the common law, which was the foundation of the auxiliary jurisdiction.

This ceased to be necessary after these Acts came into effect, because this supplement of equity was now available in every court. The conceptual foundations of the distinction between law and equity remained in place. So property lawyers continue to distinguish ownership 'at law' from ownership 'in equity', even though such distinctions are no longer reflected in differences between institutions or in divisions between jurisdictions. In this respect, the Judicature Acts simplified the 'administration of justice'. But at the same time they added a source of new complication. There were matters on which the rules of law and the rules of equity overlapped but were inconsistent. These principally occur in the area of contractual obligations, and one example must suffice. A lease, the nature of which is explored further in the next chapter, commonly today contains a rent review clause. If the lease provides a timetable for such a rent review to occur, and the timetable is not complied with, what is the position? As lawyers put it, is time, in such a context, of the essence of the contract? Law and equity diverged here in the past. The common law gave effect to the private law of the parties. If the arrangement provided a date, that was decisive. Equity's attitude, however, was different, so far as agreements which came within its purview were concerned. The practice of equity came to be that stipulations in a contract as to the time of performance would not be regarded as being of the essence unless the contract expressly said so. After the Judicature Acts, the equitable view always prevails, which means that, insofar as questions of this order are concerned, the old common law rules are effectively obsolete, and the only operative rules are those which originate from the practice of the courts of equity.

So the maxim 'Equity prevails over law' still applies. Whereas it originally resolved a jurisdictional problem between two different decision-making institutions, it means today that the equitable rules prevail if there is a conflict with the legal rules. For example, in the case of the trust, the legal rules indicate simply that the legal owner (the person with the legal estate) is entitled to the property, but the equitable rules indicate that he holds the legal estate as a trustee, that is for the benefit of someone else (who we will call the beneficiary). Thus, the legal rules say the legal owner is entitled to the property, and the rules of equity say the benefit is with the beneficiary. In this conflict of interpretation, the equitable view prevails.

EQUITABLE INTERESTS

It is against this background of the availability of equitable remedies that we can speak of equitable interests, or equitable rights. Three examples will now be considered: the 'estate contract', the 'restrictive convenant' and the 'beneficial interest behind a trust'. This order of presentation is adopted for simplicity of exposition; it is not an historical sequence of the progressive recognition of different kinds of rights by the courts of equity.

The estate contract

This is a contract between a prospective seller and a prospective purchaser of land. If the seller, having entered into the contract, later refuses to transfer the title to that land – refuses to convey the title – as he has promised, the only remedy available to the buyer at common law is a remedy in damages, financial compensation based on what the buyer has lost. But for centuries, equity has taken the view that in relation to a contract for the sale of land, damages for breach are not adequate, even though they usually are for breach of a contract to sell chattels. Because equity viewed contracts for the sale of land as special, it was prepared to decree specific performance of these contracts. It would not leave a would-be purchaser to his remedy in damages at law, but would help him to compel the seller to do what he had promised and convey the title to the land. Because the purchaser could normally (see above for the exceptions to this general rule) get specific performance of a contract to sell land, he came to be viewed as the owner of the land 'in equity' as soon as the contract was made. The legal title, of course, remained with the seller until the conveyance (the act of transfer of title) but the purchaser, because he could get specific performance against the seller, was viewed as having an equitable interest in the land. This means that the effect of the contract is in some sense to transfer certain property rights from the seller to the purchaser.

Why is it important to say not simply that the purchaser has more remedies than parties to many other kinds of contracts (because he can get specific performance) but in addition that the purchaser has an equitable interest in the land – a property right? Because, as lawyers say, third parties in certain situations will 'take subject to' these equitable interests, they have the character of property rights.

EXAMPLE V contracts with P1 to convey the title to Blackacre. V then conveys the title to P2. What is P1's position? At law, his only remedy is against V in damages for breach of contract. P1 cannot sue P2 at law on the contract because P2 is not a party to the contract and so is under no contractual duty towards P1. (This doctrine of English law, that only the parties to a contract have rights and duties under it, is known as Privity of Contract.) But in equity, P1 has an equitable interest because he could have obtained specific performance of his contract against V. In certain circumstances, P2 will be made by equity to take subject to P1's rights because P1 has an equitable interest. Under the old law, this would arise if P2 knew or 'ought' to have known (lawyers say 'had notice') of P1's rights.

What does it mean to say that P2 'takes subject to' P1's rights? The effect of the conveyance by V to P2 is to transfer the legal estate in the land from V to P2. But if P2 has notice of P1's rights, he takes subject to them. This means that P1 can pursue the same equitable (but not common law) remedies against P2 as he could have pursued against V. In short, P1 can invoke the assistance of equity against P2 and get a degree of specific performance against P2. In other words, P2 will be compelled to convey the land to P1. P2 will then be left to pursue a remedy at law against V.

The restrictive covenant

An owner (V1) of a large piece of land might sell off an outlying portion of that land to a purchaser (P1), extracting a promise known as a 'covenant' from that purchaser at the time of the conveyance that the land being sold will be used for residential purposes only. So the purchaser is promising in the covenant to limit the uses to which he may put the land. If he later goes back on this promise, that would be a breach of contract by the purchaser, and the seller could sue for damages at law in respect of that breach. But this covenant, viewed simply as a contract (that is, through common law spectacles) could have legal effect only as between the parties to the covenant. In what circumstances, if any, could the covenant have an effect if V1 sold the land he had retained to V2, and P1 sold the land he had bought to P2? Could V2 enforce the covenant against P2, if P2 proposed to use the land for non-residential purposes? Neither is a party to the covenant as a contract, and so under common law principles the covenant would be of no legal effect as between the two. But in the nineteenth century, the Court of Chancery came to give effect to the covenant in equity, and would grant the equitable remedy of the injunction to restrain breach of the covenant by P2 when its assistance was invoked by V2. Because we have now stepped well outside the common law confines of privity of contract, and relationships between non-contracting parties are being regulated by means of the injunction, we can say that V2 in this situation has a property right or equitable interest against P2. The land in P2's hands is burdened with a third-party right (V2's right to enforce the covenant).

V2, however, although he has no legal rights in P2's land, and although he has no contract with P2, has equitable rights which affect or burden P2's land. But V2's right are only equitable, and therefore if he sought to enforce them against P2, we would in the past have needed to ask if P2 knew or ought to have known (i.e. had 'notice') of the covenant. If P2 had no knowledge of the covenant made between V1 and P1, and had no way of knowing about it, the covenant would have been unenforceable by V2 against P2.

The interests of beneficiaries behind a trust

We have already seen that the trust was a creation of equity. Part of equity's jurisdiction over trustees centres around equity's jurisdiction to restrain a breach of trust. If the trustees propose to do something which is a breach of trust (for example something which is contrary to the purposes for which the trustee acquired the legal estate as legal owner, or something which, under the terms of the trust, the trustees have no power to do) then the beneficiaries can go to the court and get an injunction, by which the court will restrain the trustees from committing the breach of trust.

The jurisdiction over breaches of trust extends further. Trustees are not allowed to take a personal benefit from administering the trust. If they do, the beneficiaries can go to court to restrain the trustees from taking a personal benefit. If the beneficiaries suffer a loss as a result of the way the trust has been administered, they can go to court and get compensation from the trustees for the loss which they have suffered.

EXAMPLE T1 and T2 have the legal title to a fund, but they hold the fund as trustees. A has a life interest in possession in equity in respect of this fund, and B has a remainder in fee simple. This meant that for A's life, he was entitled to the income from the fund, and on his death, when the equitable life interest terminated, B was beneficially entitled to the capital itself – the whole fund – because his equitable fee simple – the whole beneficial interest in the trust property – had now come into possession. But during this time, legal title to the fund, and thus managerial control over it, were in the hands of trustees. The trustees were 'in charge' but were compelled by equity to deal with the fund for the benefit of the beneficiaries.

Here again, the jurisdiction may extend to people who are not formally trustees. Although the legal estate in land might be vested in P, and he would have been regarded in the common law courts as entitled to the property, equity would, under some conditions, intervene to restrain P from deriving any personal benefit from the land because of the circumstances in which P had acquired that legal estate. Equity viewed him as a legal owner who was a trustee, with obligations to a group of people who were not on the legal title, whom today we call beneficiaries.

EXAMPLE A is the legal owner of Blackacre as trustee on behalf of B and C. He transfers the legal estate to P. Does P acquire that legal estate subject to the rights of B and C or not?

In practice, this problem is only likely to arise if A runs off with the money or becomes bankrupt. Normally, if there is a difficulty, B and C will pursue their remedies against A, the trustee. But what if A is penniless (what lawyers call a man of straw)? Can they get at P? Again, under the old law, this depended on whether or not P knew or ought to have known (had notice) of the rights of B and C. If he did, then he took subject to them, and if he did not, he took free. This would mean that if B and C between them were entitled to the whole enjoyment of the property (that is, had between them the equitable fee simple in possession), then P would, if he had notice of their rights, have acquired a worthless legal estate. This would be because he would hold that legal estate he had acquired by conveyance from A as trustee for B and C, and, because they were absolutely entitled in equity to the beneficial ownership of the land, he could himself derive no benefit from the land. On the other hand, if P had no notice, he took free, and would himself as purchaser of the legal estate be absolutely entitled to the enjoyment of the land.

Since whether a purchaser took subject to equitable interests affecting the legal estate he bought depended on whether or not he had notice of these interests, equitable interests might seem to have operated as an exception to the basic principle of *nemo dat*. A, as trustee of a legal estate, was not entitled to derive any benefit from the land; the beneficial interest, in our example, is in B and C. Yet if P had no notice, these rights of beneficial ownership would not affect him. In other words, P without notice was in a better position than A, the seller, had been. This anomaly or distinction in fact highlights the different ways in which legal rights (that is, rights recognised by the common law), and equitable rights worked in the past. In asking whether a particular legal owner was affected by equitable interests in the land, equity looked at the circumstances in which the person had acquired his legal title.

EQUITY TODAY

We have already seen that before 1926 the legal fee simple absolute in possession could be split up into a number of lesser legal estates, and how the right to enjoyment of these different estates could be spread out through time (interests in possession, in remainder, reversions, etc.). The effect of the 1925 legislation was that the legal fee simple absolute in possession became the only pre-1925 freehold estate which could exist at law. The life estate and entail can today only exist in equity (i.e. behind a trust), and all future interests (i.e. interests in remainder or reversion) must also take effect in equity. Equally, all interests of tenants in common can only exist behind a trust.

Before these legislative changes, many disputes over the ownership or occupation of land could be framed in terms of the common law. The abolition of the legal life estate in particular means that contemporary disputes have to be framed at the level of equity, in terms of implied trusts or, more generally, 'equities'. So in a nineteenth-century case, a housekeeper who claimed that she had a right to remain for the rest of her life in the house where she had lived and worked after her employer had died, and whom his heirs were trying to remove, resorted to the jurisdiction of equity merely in the old way, for remedial assistance. What she sought was a legal life estate, arguing that she had an equity to get one through a decree of the court.[10] In the modern world, any such person must not just make a case for equitable intervention, through establishing an equity in the old sense of the word, but must also conceptualise in the language of equity the substantive nature of the right to which he or she is laying claim. As we shall see, many of the 'new' equitable interests are not new in substance, but they are new first in that they operate 'in equity' and not 'at law'. Secondly, they are new in that they arise informally and do not originate in formal documents nor can their continued existence be so proved. Although it is often repeated that equity looks not to form but to substance, it must be stressed that this informal character of the 'new' equities is not connected with the fact that these rights are equitable. (As we see in the next chapter, the common law was long familiar with dealing with entirely informal tenancies, and much of the work of courts of equity, over a long period of time, centred around the construction of formal documents like trust instruments and wills, and remains so today.) Rather, informality derives from the circumstances which generate the disputes. We return to this in the final chapter, where the idea of form and substance in English land law is reappraised. We conclude this chapter by looking more closely at the first aspect of what is new, the fact that the framework of the 1925 code forces many disputes concerning land to be couched in the language of equity rather than the language of law.

The 1925 code transformed the conceptual scheme within which disputes about the ownership or occupation of land could be framed; quite different factors transformed what such disputes, in substance, could be about. The principal focus of the discussion is housing. The first point is the rise of public housing in this century. Because of the capital expenditure involved in house building programmes, this has constituted one of the axes on which relations between central and local government have hinged. But so long as such housing remains in the public sector, it cannot generate disputes which impinge upon the lawyer's understanding of what property is. Transfers of council tenancies, and succession to tenancies on the death of the existing tenant, are all matters for specific, statutory schemes and local authority policies. The rise of this housing sector coincides with the decline in the relative significance of the private rented sector. Because this sector embraces some of the acutest manifestations of social deprivation in modern Britain, it has understandably been the focus of intensive study by progressive lawyers. But its significance for the development of the law of property since the enactment of the 1925 code has been negligible by comparison with the explosion of the owner-occupied housing sector, the sector whose contextual importance has been only enhanced by recent government policies promoting the sale of council houses to their tenants (see Murphy and Clark, 1983: 1–13; and Swenarton and Taylor, 1985).

These contextual changes can now be combined with the conceptual reorganisation brought in by the 1925 code and the enhanced role of equity within it. Against the background of mortgage-financed owner-occupation, the range of probable disputes relating to housing in this sector is fairly limited. Principally they concern either the ownership or occupation of residential property, and for the most part arise on marital or quasi-marital breakdown or on death. Since 1925, the legal owner of the property must either have an estate in fee simple or a leasehold estate, the nature of which is elaborated in the next chapter. A dispute at law can only arise between legal joint tenants, where for example a couple are joint owners of their home and are both on the title. In such circumstances, the principal kind of dispute which can find its way to a court is over sale of the house, in respect of which question the courts now have a broad discretion conferred by statute to make such order as they think fit. In marital or quasi-marital disputes, a legal analysis of the relationship in terms of landlord and tenant is more or less obsolete, for reasons outlined in the next chapter. All other attempts to assert rights of ownership or occupation are necessarily pushed either into the domain of equity or into the (legal) province of contract.

All these changes boil down to two things for the development of land law in recent years. First, the legal life estate has had, in effect, to be reinvented, through the conceptual resources available to modern lawyers. Because of the changes brought in by legislation in 1925, this reinvention has been forced to occur in equity. Secondly, lawyers have had to find a way of defining the basis upon which people other than those on the title can establish a claim to a share in the fruits of owner-occupation.

We conclude by outlining, in turn, each of these accommodations, beginning with the second. This came first because, until the 1970s, the courts had to apply the 'general principles' of property law to marital breakdown. And because of the changes in the context of such disputes, since one of the things which required resolution on marital breakdown was the ownership of the matrimonial home, there was pressure, at the level of equity, to specify the circumstances in which people acquired ownership rights in equity even if they had none at law, that is, were not on the legal title to the house or flat in question. Change in context, in brief, led to change in text. But the text was not that of the conveyancer but that of the judge. This is what was new. If the conveyancer's context had always been social relations, the judge's context had traditionally been the text prepared by the conveyancer. The 1925 legislation was assembled on the basis of just such a scheme of things. But now this changed: it was social relations themselves, unmediated by the conveyancer's text, which served as the context – the object – of judicial activity. Judges now had to interpret the world of everyday life, without assistance from the specialists in the business of formalising inheritance and transfer by sale. That their own 'prejudices' thus became more transparent, that they were forced to resort to drawing upon their own understandings as to the meaning of action in the social world, was inevitable. Inevitably too such transformations led to confusion, because judges were called upon to deal with matters of which they had no deep experience and therefore no framework within which to proceed. It would, however, have been scandalous to admit this directly, which is why, even given clear signs of unease which are manifest in the written record of decisions, the judges, as living oracles of the law, were constrained to present the decisions which they made as consistent with the tradition (when they were not), or as 'adaptations' of principle when they were departures. This is another reason why land law is difficult for the student; judicial decisions continually rewrite legal history without admitting it.

The reformulation of ownership rights in equity

Once trusts were recognised by the courts of equity, they came to be formalised and elaborated by conveyancers, although they rarely rivalled the strict settlement of land in complexity and intricacy of composition. But trusts of this type – which we call 'express trusts' because they are deliberately created, with the help of lawyers, in the social world – could also serve as a model permitting the equity courts to extend the reach of their remedies. Equity came to impose trusts upon legal estates, justifying such imposition with reference to the circumstances in which those who held these estates had acquired them. There were several instances of this but only one concerns us here. This is what is called the 'resulting trust'. Where land was conveyed to a nominee and the purchase price paid by another who intended no gift to the nominee, equity would impose a resulting trust upon the nominal purchaser of the estate in favour of the 'real' purchaser, looking to the 'substance' of the purchase (the source of the money) rather than to the 'form' of the conveyance.

The resulting trust provided the most accessible device for modelling the analysis of disputes about ownership of the matrimonial home, when that was necessary. It is less important today, in property disputes between married couples, because the courts now have statutory powers to vary the property rights of spouses on divorce or judicial separation. But where the disputants, whatever the precise nature of their relationship, are not married, it remains the principal mechanism for framing a dispute about ownership. The difficulty which courts have experienced centres upon specifying the boundary conditions for its deployment.

The difficulty in adapting the resulting trust to modern conditions is rooted in changes in practices of land purchase. It was not uncommon for people in the past, as we see in the next chapter, to finance the purchase of land by borrowing money secured upon a mortgage of the purchased land. What is different is the manner in which such loans are repaid. The legal framework within which judges of the past worked and around which the 1925 code was organised took the servicing of the loan out of rental income as its operational model. Indeed, as we shall see, repayment of the borrowed capital was in one sense not fundamental to the mortgage device, which was equally a way of securing the entitlement to interest upon the capital advanced. Now it is different. Building societies and banks, who lend money for the purchase of houses or flats, do so on the basis that the money lent will be repaid along with interest, within a period of time indicated in advance. In most cases, moreover, it is assumed that the repayments will be made from the earned income of the borrower. This in turn means that the mortgage repayments simply form part of the outgoings of a household, along with the bills for gas and electricity, telephone, and food. Put simply, then, the problem is the difficulty, in life and therefore in a dispute about ownership, of separating contributions to the repayment of the mortgage loan from other household outgoings. And since the practice of lenders has tended in the direction of refusing, or being reluctant, to lend a sum equal to the whole purchase price, most purchaser-borrowers have had to find a deposit for the purchase price. However people arrange their affairs, there is always room for argument, along one of the lines suggested above, that someone who is not on the title is entitled in equity to a share of the value of the property. There are a number of reasons why people with a claim in equity to be recognised as owners might not have their names on the legal title. Once again, such reasons spring more from life than from law.

The courts have come to impose a resulting trust today where there is an 'actual common intention' that the claimant should have a share of the property and where, secondly, the claimant has made direct or indirect contribution towards the costs of acquisition. What the first requirement means is not exactly clear. As formulated, it seems to conflate the traditional ground for imposing a trust of this kind – the generation of an 'equity' through the payment of purchase money – with the quite different idea of agreement providing the basis for equitable intervention, a frame of reference, in other words, which is very close to the idea of a contract. But the main function of this requirement seems to be that it provides a way of excluding claims where, upon close analysis of the particular facts, the court concludes that no share was intended. Conversely, where the most plausible interpretation of the facts is that a share was intended, 'actual common intention' provides a superficially attractive catchphrase to justify the imposition of a trust upon the legal owner.

The second requirement, which does seem to echo the traditional rationale of the resulting trust, is perhaps best understood as an attempt to draw a line somewhere and in that sense as a general guideline for the judicial processing of disputes. It is generally accepted today that monetary contributions will be recognised and result in the 'award' of an interest in the event of a dispute. There are a few cases, all somewhat unusual, which suggest that exceptional work on a property can lead to a similar award. But 'ordinary' domestic labour – maintenance and repair, and childrearing – has usually been excluded. Inevitably, such decisions can be seen as underpinned by a certain 'ideology', and inevitably too, the rhetoric of 'direct or indirect contribution' can be interpreted as a means of rationalising a distinction between claims which the judiciary wish to uphold and those which they do not. But from the point of view of judicial administration, the central difficulty, in this relatively uncharted area, is how to achieve at least the appearance of consistency in decision-making. That every dispute in this area requires some kind of line to be drawn is obvious enough; it does not follow that judges are willing to admit that this accurately characterises the enterprise in which they are engaged.

Because the courts now have statutory powers to make property adjustments on divorce which override the principles of property law introduced here, the resulting trust is principally relevant, in a marital relationship, where there is a dispute between the couple and a third party, as in the case where a bank or building society seeks possession of the house because they have defaulted on the mortgage repayments.

Lifetime rights

There is a duality – indeed an ambivalence – which lies at the centre of the English lawyer's way of thinking about rights to land less than full, absolute, ownership. As stressed above, the 'enjoyment' of land can take two forms: receipt of the rent which land generates or physical enjoyment of the land. If 'land' means a house, you can rent it out and pocket the income or live in it yourself. This duality is not peculiar to land. Exactly the same could be said, for example, about a trust of an old master, under which someone had, for his or her life, the right to hang the picture at home but not the right to sell it and receive the proceeds of the sale. But the disputes of recent years which have found their way to the courts, and thus called for a response, have not, for the most part, been about pictures but about houses, and, in particular, about specifying the conditions in which people who live in houses which belong to others can continue to live in them for the duration of their lives, or, at least, for as long as they wish.

In the nineteenth century, most people were tenants of or lodgers in the houses they inhabited. Not so with owner-occupation. People who live in houses which belong to other people are more likely to be living there because of some social relationship with the owner which, in the event of a dispute, must be identified from a spectrum which spans relatives, lovers, and people who are simply buying a house together without any sexual or emotional involvement with one another. There have been a large number of reported decisions in this area and a proliferation of conceptual tools for the analysis of such disputes. Thus we find counsel presenting arguments or judges analysing facts in terms of 'contractual licence', 'personal licence', 'equitable licence', 'equity', 'proprietary estoppel' or just 'estoppel', and 'constructive trust'. In one case, the owner tries to get a possession order against the occupant and is denied the order because the occupant has an equitable licence to remain. In another, the owner, the court says, is estopped from evicting the occupant becaue of 'equities' which arise in the occupant's favour. This causes anxiety to a student, since, by any yardstick of legal 'relevance', it seems impossible to see what in the facts of the two cases justifies the deployment of different analytical tools. The answer is perhaps to distinguish between the superficial – and trivial – difference in labels and the underlying continuity in substantive approach. Labelling differences are merely symptomatic of the fact that these kinds of disputes are relatively new and different judges are trying to find a preferred way of talking them through.

Beneath these differences are straightforward differences in circumstances. On the one hand, there are occupants who claim the right to remain based on agreement, whether or not they pay 'rent' to the owner. These can be called contractual licences, though they are not invariably. As we see in Chapter 8, such arrangements are now generally regarded as equitable interests capable of binding third parties like purchasers and mortgagees. Imposition of a 'contractual' tag upon the relationship requires of course something in the facts which can count as consideration to support the promise moving from the owner that the occupant can remain. Sometimes this is impossible, though often it is not, because if the occupant does housework or keeps the garden in order, that can, if the court wishes, be treated as consideration. But more generally, a contractual label may 'feel' inappropriate because the relationship between the parties has shifted and drifted over time, is too diffuse, in other words, to be called an 'agreement'. Here, estoppel or constructive trust sometimes seem to provide more comfortable means of arriving at lifetime rights, especially where the facts are amenable to the conclusion that the occupant has acted to his or her detriment on the understanding that occupation could continue indefinitely. What counts as 'detriment' is also a matter for the judgement of the court. We have been told that payment of money is not necessary, and that 'lost opportunities' will suffice. Yet it is inescapable that one judge presents as a matter of contract what another presents as a matter of 'equity' or trust. Finally, we should note that this barrage of concepts is not confined to the formulation of lifetime rights but of rights of occupation generally. But it is chiefly in the context of relatively elderly defendants, seeking to remain in occupation of property belonging to someone else, that the higher courts have had to resolve these disputes. This is why it has tended to be the case that successful defendants have been permitted to remain for the rest of their lives.

It is difficult to assess the importance of such indeterminacy in the present practice of the courts. There is nothing new about the judicial attempt to preserve 'leeway' or room for manoeuvre. All that changes is where such flexibility needs to be sought at any point in time. But for the law student, oppressed by the need to distill from the cases an analytical certainty usable in the examination room, the deeply engrained pragmatism of English law can be frustrating, even disturbing.

The judicial desire to keep things vague is not new, but where it is sought is. In matters concerning property, and especially title to land, leeway hovered in the margins of formal documents of title. That all these products of the new vagueness, these diffuse rights generated by contract or by 'equity', are capable of binding purchasers of land would probably not have surprised a nineteenth-century conveyancer, as we shall see. But that such rights could come into existence without any formality, and yet amount to a right to enjoy land for life, would have seemed bizarre, and dangerous. Occupants whose rights rested solely on the fact of their occupation, and whose rights did not rest upon legal formulae inscribed on paper, were perfectly familiar to conveyancers. They were the tenants and lodgers mentioned above. But their rights were short-term and relatively fragile in strict legal terms. In the nineteenth-century conveyancer's frame of reference, lifetime rights of occupation were formalised into legal life estates or into leases for lives. That was how things were done. And as we shall see, the 1925 legislation was constructed on the basis that things were done as they should be.

5

Tenancies, Leases and Mortgages

So far we have outlined the principal ways in which, in the past, title to land could be fragmented in English law, and indicated the general strategy pursued in 1925 for overcoming the complexities which these practices of fragmentation generated for the transfer of title. The machinery adopted to implement this strategy, and the reasons why what was adopted was chosen, are examined in later chapters. First we must introduce a further range of property interests, which from one point of view can be regarded as 'encumbrances' upon a title. That is, we are concerned with a range of 'rights', which, in the English lawyer's scheme of things, are property rights and not mere contractual or personal rights, since they possess some of the attributes of durability and transmissibility singled out above, but which in some way or other amount to something 'less' than the 'unqualified' right of enjoyment which lawyers have associated with holding an unencumbered freehold estate in land.

In this chapter, we consider tenancies, leases, which are a particular form of tenancy, and mortgages, which can, in the modern law, take the form of a lease. In the following chapter we consider a number of rights and liabilities which can be latched on to titles, to benefit them or to encumber them, all of which concern the manner in which landowners are entitled to use the land which they own.

Attention has already been drawn to the historical importance of the rent relation. As we have said, most of the varied forms which the relation assumed in the past have now been eclipsed. What remains is the tenancy. Rent is not an essential ingredient of what lawyers mean by a tenancy although almost invariably the relation between landlord and tenant will involve the payment of rent by the tenant to the landlord. But what does the lawyer mean by 'rent'? It is the 'annual profit arising out of lands and tenements corporeal', a

99

profit which can, and usually does, consist of money, 'or of money's worth, as, for example, of arms, horses, corn, or of other things' (Bullen, 1899: 20). Rent 'must issue out of the land, and not be part of the land itself; so that the grass, herbage, or other vesture cannot properly constitute a rent.' Rent is the reservation of a thing 'not in being', 'to be newly created or produced out of the land or tenement demised' (ibid.). These distinctions between being and non-being are perhaps the closest English lawyers, with their reluctance for 'speculation', came to articulating the metaphysical undercore of their thought.

TENANCIES AND LEASES

A tenancy could perhaps be called a 'temporary' ownership right: 'ownership' in the sense that, while it lasts, the tenant has exclusive use of the property, 'temporary' in the sense that at some time in the future these rights will cease and the right to possess and enjoy the land will revert to the landlord. Secondly, as we shall see, a tenancy is a form of 'conditional' ownership, in that the relationship between landlord and tenant usually involves obligations which impose duties on both parties relating to the manner in which the tenant may enjoy the property during the time that he has exclusive possession of it.

Of all the interests in land considered in this book, the tenancy is the most difficult to classify by means of the distinction between fragmentation of and encumbrance upon title. There are two reasons for this. First, it is a matter of perspective: it all depends on which way you look at it. A lawyer whose client wants to buy a landlord's title views a tenancy as an encumbrance on the title he has to investigate for his purchaser. It is an interest adverse to the title he wants to buy; it limits the enjoyment of the land by the person who has the title, and the lawyer's task is to investigate the extent of that limit. By contrast, a lawyer whose client wants to buy the tenancy approaches the tenancy as a title in its own right. His concern here will be primarily to ascertain the extent of the enjoyment afforded by the tenancy viewed as a title, and the conditions attached to that enjoyment. Secondly, the 'temporary' nature of the relationship between landlord and tenant varies considerably, depending upon the nature of the arrangement upon which both have embarked. Some tenancies, in a practical sense, are much more like titles in their own right than others. If we cease to view the opposition between fragmentation of title and encumbrance on title as a rigid either/or, and dissolve the opposition into a spectrum of possibilities, we can say that tenancies range from being very close to absolute ownership, in a practical sense, to being very minor and temporary encumbrances upon title.

The extent of the involvement of lawyers in the creation of a relationship between landlord and tenant varied considerably in the past. In some cases, their stylized drafting skills were lavishly deployed in formalising the relationship. But in many other cases tenancies were completely informal, without lawyers being involved in their formation or their subsequent course. Such tenancies, from the practical point of view of the lawyer, were essentially encumbrances on the landlord's title, things to be checked out on a transfer of that title, and, it should be added, encumbrances of a type which were readily observable and which caused relatively little difficulty in practice. We will see later that it was the existence of formal tenancies as encumbrances on the landlord's title which presented more difficulty from the conveyancing point of view. In modern conditions, the growth of various regimes of regulation of landlord-tenant relationships has increased the involvement of lawyers – and the degree of formalisation – in most of these relationships.

The 'lease' is a 'formalised' tenancy. It is this device which lawyers have in mind when they describe a tenancy as a 'term of years absolute'. It is leases rather than tenancies in general which are often best grasped as an instance of fragmentation of title. In the past, indeed, the lease really was another way of carving 'lesser' interests out of the largest interest, the fee simple. Such leases could be carved up in exactly the same way as fee simples, as where leases were granted for successive lives, especially by the Church of England and by some colleges in Oxford and Cambridge. And this is why, in 1925, it was provided that the only legal estate in land which could exist in the future, alongside the fee simple absolute in possession, was the term of years absolute, i.e. the lease.

The legal concept of a lease involves two principal requirements. First, for a valid lease to be created, it must give to the lessee exclusive possession of the land or buildings which are the subject matter of the lease. 'Exclusive possession' means, principally, possession exclusive of the lessor, and is the yardstick for distinguishing a leasehold estate from a lesser right, from easements in particular, as we see in the next chapter. Secondly, it is said, the maximum duration of the lease – the term which it creates – must be known at the outset if a valid lease is to be created. So instruments purporting to grant leases of buildings in London 'for the duration of the [Second World] War' were held not to create legal leases,[11] but mere tenancies terminable at short notice by the landlord. Finally, it is provided by statute that an instrument under seal is required to create a term valid at law of over three years.

A lease is a conveyance of title. Therefore, much of what needs to be said about the 'law' of leases is discussed below when the role of lawyers in the management of transfers of title to land is examined. Moreover, it is obvious that in practical terms, a very long lease – say for 999 years – is at first sight a conveyance of title not much different from that obtained by a conveyance of a fee simple. (We will see in due course, however, that there is a difference which will normally arise in practice, because, while a lease must have a maximum duration, it need not have a minimum duration. There are a range of ways in which leases can terminate ahead of time, which is rarely the case – though not impossible – in a conveyance of a fee simple.)

In this century, a substantial body of functionally differentiated statute law has grown up around the landlord-tenant relationship, such that today the nineteenth-century rules have limited – though still very important – practical application. But to get the subject as a whole into perspective, it is necessary to look back to the past. In historical terms, the landlord-tenant relationship is, perhaps, from a social as well as legal point of view, the most important one examined in this book. While all lessees are tenants, not all tenants are lessees. The formal definitional rules stated above apply to all tenants, if a little artificially, but they are really formulated with lessees in mind. We can clarify this by examining the legal and social historical contexts of the relationship.

The principal contextual distinction is between the rural and urban sectors, or, slightly differently as we shall see, between agricultural land – farms – and housing. What follows is necessarily overgeneralized, because there were considerable regional differences in landholding forms, but it does delineate a framework which many people used to think did hold generally true, and on the basis of which assumption the regulatory framework of the twentieth century has been constructed.

The rural context: farms[12]

Our discussion of settlements of land above stressed that what was fundamentally being provided for in such settlements was the distribution of rents through time among family members. Some of these rents – in many cases, the bulk of them – took the form of agricultural or farm rents. The 'broad acres' of a landed estate were in fact composed of a number of farms, each yielding a rent paid by the tenant farmer who worked the farm. Until changes which came in the wake of the First World War, in which the scions of landed families fell alongside the sons of tenant farmers in the trenches by the Somme, such tenancies, to judge from the evidence, commonly remained in one farming family over several generations. But such tenancies were very often extremely informal, as those devoted to the cause of improving the state of agriculture in England emphasised with growing intensity from the middle of the nineteenth century. Why?

People of the time called these farming tenancies 'tenancies at will', as do today's historians. Strictly, lawyers call them yearly periodic tenancies. But the same thing is meant by both, for a simple reason: the legal conceptualisation of these relationships was largely a matter of clothing fact with right. The landowner could terminate the tenancy at his pleasure, but, given the nature of farming, at pleasure would normally mean giving notice on certain days of the year, and allowing the tenant six months, principally in order to gather such crops as he may have planted. At one level this meant that the exiguous legal structure of this relationship afforded much social power to the landowner, whose ability to terminate the tenancy at pleasure might hang like a sword of Damocles over the heads of his tenant farmers. But the legal relationship was for the most part enveloped in a broader normative framework, as well as being underpinned by the brute fact of mutual dependency. The landowner, in many cases, was principally interested in his rental income. In a time of severe agricultural depression, for example, the landlord might do better to allow his tenant farmers to go into arrears rather than exercise his legal rights, in the hope that over time things would balance out. Resident landlords, who had to coexist over time with their tenants, were likely to be particularly subject to these diffuse normative pressures. This, more than anything, was perhaps the problem underlying absentee landlords, most notably in Ireland. An English landowner's Irish estates were, all too often, merely a source of rental income and not in any larger, more normative sense the fulcrum of a set of face-to-face social relationships, in which legal rights, social norms and political power were all interwoven in a largely undifferentiated way.

The modern regulatory scheme springs principally from the problems of Ireland. It is interesting to note that legislation was required, because, as said above, mid-nineteenth-century reformers thought that most of what was needed could be achieved by formalizing the relationship by means of a lease. Let us return to why they thought this to be so.

Informal tenancies were largely governed by traditional localised norms, so that lawyers were commonly faced with a *fait accompli*. But in the nature of things, these norms might be rather diffuse and vague. As between landowner and tenant farmer, rights and duties might not always be clearly spelt out. People interested in agricultural improvement in the nineteenth century – in improving farming methods, in increasing the potential yield of land and in methods of improving the manner of storage of its produce – saw the formal lease as a mechanism for spelling out in advance precisely who was responsible for what, and for enshrining in legal terms how the land was to be utilised. Those who advocated the adoption of leases hoped, by formalising all this, to focus the minds of the parties at the time of entering into the transaction. The traditional tenancy, because of its informal character, was seen as an obstacle to improvement in these respects. Moreover, its vagueness, it was said, enveloped the tenant farmer with a cluster of disincentives. Given that only a sense of 'fair play', and not the law, deterred the landowner from terminating the relationship at will, what incentive was there for the tenant farmer to engage in agricultural improvement? Why should he build barns, drain land, clear wasteland and so on, if his landlord could turn him out at any time and reap the benefit of the improvement himself? These questions, which were posed with most intensity in the Irish context, because, on the whole, absentee landlords behaved that much worse, shaped the form taken by legislative interventions. A regime providing some security of tenure was laid down (see now principally the Agricultural Holdings Act 1948 as amended); and provision was made for 'tenant right', whereby the tenant farmer could be compensated on the termination of his tenancy for improvements made during his time. Both could largely have been accommodated through the adoption of formal leases; that they were not was largely due to inertia. In the face of inertia, a general legislative framework was established.

The urban context: housing[13]

It is even harder to generalize with any accuracy about the legal forms through which the occupation of houses was arranged. The most that can be said at present is that the arrangements which we now examine were common in some towns, cities or regions, and that these forms, whether real or merely perceived by legislators and reformers, have left their imprint upon the framework of the present law.

Whatever the position in remoter times, when most people lived in the country, the urbanisation of England in the nineteenth century meant, among other things, that farmland adjacent to what were once small towns became the target of urban development. People who owned such land at the time that pressure for development came upon it – whether industrial or residential; indeed, obviously, the two went together – were faced with two choices. They could sell the land to a developer. But such a course of action would involve the problem of alternative safe places for the proceeds of sale. So the course which was widely adopted was not to sell up entirely but to grant leases of land wanted for development. Such leases would draw upon all the expertise of lawyers, and contain detailed plans for how the land let to the builder should be built upon. Lawyers called these leases 'building leases', which were typically of sixty or ninety years' duration. Under such leases, the builder/developer would be responsible for erecting a building or a number of buildings upon a particular site, and detailed provision might be made for the manner of their construction and continuing maintenance, even down to the type of subsequent letting of the buildings which was to be permitted. The lease would reserve a 'ground rent' for the land-owner. Relative to the rental income which the building, once constructed, could yield to the builder, or the capital value of the lease if he sold it on (see below), this ground rent would constitute a small amount per annum. From the landowner's financial point of view, its significance lay simply in the fact that, by comparison with the yield which could be derived from agricultural land, urbanised exploitation was a much more intensive form of exploitation so far as revenue generation was concerned. The broad acres of rural England might be replaced by stretches of suburbia which seem to us to epitomise England, or, for that matter, by tenements which, in their way, also do: the ground rent for each parcel might be small, but such a process of development permitted many more such rents to be created. When agricultural rents came under pressure in the 1880s, it was those landowners who owned many ground rents who best withstood the storm. But for them to be really valuable, you had to have a lot of them. A few families did. By contrast with the manner in which landowners were unconcerned to encase their rental incomes from farmland in the guarantees of the law, their urban rental incomes from ground rents were wrapped up in as much law as you could get at the time. But what happened to these buildings, once constructed?

The speculative, 'capitalist' builder was faced with a choice of his own. He could sell on the term (as lawyers say, 'assign' it). Or he could rent out the property. If he sold on, the capital value would be assessed in relation to the potential future rental yield, in the light of the outstanding term of the lease. As we shall see, it is all different today.

So in the urban context we encounter two rental incomes generated from the same physical entity: the ground rent and the house or occupancy rent, whether actual – because the house is let out – or notional – that is, a rent which serves simply as a measure for calculating the capital value of the lease.

In a practical sense, then, there were two different things which could be 'owned' over a long period of time: the ground rent on the one hand, the building on the other, which is why you find lawyers at the time talking about house owners when the interest is in fact leasehold and subject to the payment of ground rent.

When we come to the nature of the position of those using such houses or buildings as residences, it is necessary to draw distinctions, however roughly, in terms of social class, as people did at the time. Broadly, middle-class families considered it sensible to embark on formal leases, though often of fairly short duration, in much the same way, no doubt, as it is thought sensible today for anyone with a job to buy a house or flat. In many industrialised parts of the country, working-class housing, by contrast, was primarily arranged through informal weekly tenancies, in principle determinable on the giving of one week's notice by either side. Rent books recording payment (or non-payment) of rent came to be used by rent collectors, which served as evidence of the tenancy and, more importantly, could serve as a testimonial for a 'good' tenant seeking a tenancy from a new landlord (Dennis, 1984: 170). In the twentieth century, legislation has made such rent books mandatory.

The shape of the present regulatory framework, mainly derived from statute, arises, as we have said, largely from these practices of the past. In 1917 the War Cabinet sought to keep down the wages of its munitions workers through a statutory regime controlling the rents which landlords could charge their tenants, and the interest rates which mortgagees (i.e. lenders on mortgage) could charge their borrowers (that is, in terms of the assumptions of the time, landlords of working-class houses who had borrowed money on mortgages secured on the houses that they owned). This statutory scheme protecting tenants survived the war more or less permanently, though some governments have sought, prospectively, to 'decontrol' rents, and their successors to reimpose controls.

Statutory control has two principal elements: public control of the level of rent and security of tenure for the tenant. Public officials have been empowered to set rent levels for a particular property if so requested by either landlord or tenant (though the precise criteria such officials are to use have varied over time) and statutes have imposed a range of limits upon the landlords' ability to regain possession of the rented property, at the end of the contracted term, through the judicial process.

The details of this history are beyond our present scope; with one exception, this can be regarded as a quite separate body of statute law, throwing up the usual problems of statutory interpretation for the courts, but with minimal impact, despite its practical significance, for the general fabric of English land law. This is signalled in the terminology which lawyers use today in describing tenancies which come within one or other of these statutory regimes: the 'contractual' tenancy is contrasted with the 'statutory' tenancy, which indicates the contrast between the relationship actually bargained for – say a one-year tenancy taken by a group of students – and the relationship imposed upon the parties by the statutory scheme, which comes into effect when the 'contractual' tenancy expires.

There has been much debate over whether the imposition of such statutory controls is directly responsible for the overall decline in the private rented housing sector, though this decline is in any case unevenly distributed across the country. Rent control is a disincentive only if, first, the officials controlling rents set them at uneconomic levels. What is 'uneconomic' depends, secondly, upon what alternative opportunities are available for investment in urban land, and a comparison of the returns from such investments with the returns from alternative sources of investment such as shares. To the extent that the substance of litigation can serve as an indicator to what is the major disincentive (and here, as anywhere else in the law, that is very problematic), it is security of tenure which has most troubled private landlords, and which has led to attempts to find ways of circumventing statutory control. This is not surprising. From the landlord's point of view, rent control affects the level of income that land will yield; any established system of official decision-making on rent levels within a particular town or region will, over time, enable permissible rent levels to become relatively predictable and therefore calculable in advance. But security of tenure is not so calculable, it involves a level of contingency analogous to that involving certain kinds of leases in the past.

Suppose in the past someone bought a freehold estate which was subject to a lease for two successive lives. The price would take account of the rent reserved under the lease, and the contingency that 'full' enjoyment of the land by the purchaser would depend on the duration of the lives in question. The purchaser took a gamble: if the lives were long-lived, his freehold would remain in reversion for a long period; if both died soon after the purchase, the lease would quickly be at an end and the purchaser would then be free to sell unencumbered. The effect of security of tenure imposed by statute is broadly the same, with the added contingency, operating in the landlord's favour, that the tenant might decide to move out and thereby terminate the statutory protection of the tenancy.

In their nature, the old leases for lives were voluntarily created by an owner of the estate at some point in time. By contrast, their modern equivalents are imposed by statute, and where statute imposes, owners of property often endeavour, with the help of their lawyers, to find a way around the imposition. So the attempt was made to find ways through which residential property could be exploited commercially to yield an income without the label of 'landlord and tenant' being attached by the courts to the relationship between owner and resident. This led, in other words, to pressure upon the definition of the concept of 'tenancy' in English law.

Initially, the question was presented in terms of the distinction between commercial and non-commercial, especially 'family', arrangements. If someone 'let' his brother live in a house which he owned, in return for the payment of a weekly sum of money, the courts described the arrangement as a contractual licence not a tenancy, with the result that statutory control did not apply. This approach, however, suggested that any commercial arrangement would fall within the statutory scheme, at least where, under the arrangement, the resident obtained, in fact or by express agreement, exclusive possession of the premises in question. This led in turn to a greater formalisation of commercial residential lettings, where the principal 'technical' aim was to construct an agreement under which the resident would not be permitted exclusive possession of the property. These were, and are, known as 'non-exclusive occupation' agreements, under which the landlord purports to reserve the right to confer the right to possession of the premises upon someone other than the contracting residents. The effect of these agreements has been much litigated, and a recent decision of the House of Lords has held that the crucial question for the courts to ask in interpreting them is whether, taking all the elements of the actual relationship into account, the resident is in practice a lodger, being supplied with services by the landlord, or a tenant with exclusive occupation. If the latter, then the relationship is within the scheme of statutory control. Put in other terms, the lower courts have been urged to view with suspicion these blatant attempts at avoiding statutory control, and to concentrate upon the substance rather than the form of the transaction between owner and resident.

LEASES AND LAWYERS

Three principal sets of questions have exercised lawyers regarding the contents of a lease and their legal consequences. The first set concerns what should be put in a lease and the manner in which these should be formalised. The second involves the question how a lease can be terminated, which in turn divides into two different scenarios: the mechanisms available for consensual termination on the one hand, termination 'ahead of time' as an additional remedial device for landlords on the other. The third concerns the legal effect of the contents of a lease once either landlord or tenant transfers his interest to another.

It must first be stressed that the contents of a lease constitute a kind of 'private' law, where lawyers create the regime to which landlord and tenant are to be subject. Here as more generally with the preparation of the transfer documentation, the expertise of the lawyer is essentially formulaic. The courts have had very little to do with setting the terms of the relationship, although legislative intervention has now made a difference in certain areas. No general rights and duties can usefully be said to be imposed by common law upon the landlord-tenant relationship as such, though a very small number are in specific, rather narrowly drawn contexts. The common law tradition must be understood as essentially abstentionist in this area. It is for the parties to create their private law.

From this point of view, the repairing covenant is perhaps the most important item in a lease. Buildings in the English climate are prone to all kinds of dilapidation. Wherever there is a lease, good legal sense suggests that attention should be given to the allocation of responsibility for repairs and maintenance of the fabric of the building. If you look at the pages of the specialist books on landlord and tenant, acres of words are devoted to the subject of repair. Nearly all of this learning is concerned, at bottom, with the question of formulae. What forms of words will make the lessor or the lessee responsible for renewing the roof or the windows and so on? It is not a matter of law versus policy, rather a matter of style.

This needs to be borne in mind when we follow through the course of a dispute over repairs into an area where it is easy to get the impression that the courts do have room to be active because they have statutory discretion, and where, therefore, it might be thought that 'justice' has a role to play.

In a lease of any significant duration, the repair obligations are commonly placed upon the lessee, whether the lease be of commercial premises or of residential property. The precise form these repair obligations take varies, as does their extent. Specifying the parts of the building to which they extend is essentially a matter of the formulae, and that is why so much learning on the subject is described in the lawbooks. Once, however, the answer to that is ascertained – and often there will be no room for argument because the lessor's lawyer has done his job properly (or put the other way round, if there is, he has not) – the role of the court is simply to enforce the covenant where the lessee allows the building to fall into disrepair. Directly, the court hears an action for, and then awards, damages. Indirectly, though, the lawyer who drafted the lease may have attached to the covenants in the lease a clause stating that failure to perform the covenants entitles the landlord to re-enter. That is, what is called a forfeiture clause has been put in the lease. If the tenant fails to perform, the landlord can go to court and seek to repossess the premises.

This process of repossession or forfeiture has been regulated by statute in two ways since 1925. So far as repair covenants are concerned, this gives the lessee two opportunities to 'repent', as a court has put it recently.[14] First, section 146 of the Law of Property Act 1925 requires the lessor to serve a forfeiture notice on the lessee and to require the breach of covenant – here, the failure to repair – to be remedied if it is capable of remedy. The courts have now interpreted this to mean that the lessor must require remedy of the breach if in a practical sense the landlord can be put back into the position he would have been in had the tenant not defaulted on his obligations. If the landlord serves such a notice and the tenant does the repairs, then the breach is in effect cured and the tenant can remain. But if he does not remedy the breach, the landlord can repossess unless the court grants the tenant relief against forfeiture.

The basis of this jurisdiction to grant relief matters little at present. What matters is rather to explore what lawyers suppose to be the proper function of the court when the jurisdiction is invoked. The courts do not wave sabres of justice at this point. The lessor, via his lawyer, has laid down in the lease a private law for the premises. The courts tend to approach this private law with circumspection; that is, they are there to facilitate its implementation, not to rewrite it. This is what is expected from them by practitioners. Such expectations form the basis of what practitioners do when they draw up leases, as well as when, in the background for the formation of a private law, they advise on the likely outcome of a lawsuit. A lessee who has deliberately broken the terms of his lease, or refused to remedy his breach, is extremely unlikely to succeed if he appeals to a court to relieve him from the consequences.

The first opportunity for a lessee to save himself is by remedying the breach and this opportunity, we have just seen, the statute requires him to be given. But it only arises where the breach is capable of being remedied. Some breaches are not, it has been decided (notably breaches of covenant which forbid assignments or sublettings of the lease without permission from the lessor). In such circumstances, tenants involved in forfeiture proceedings can never save themselves from the landlord except by availing themselves of the relief jurisdiction, by throwing themselves upon the mercy of the court. And here, precisely because remediability is ruled out of court, there is scope for seeking relief. If the breach cannot be remedied, but is innocent or innocuous, relief may be granted. The tenant then gets relief because at worst he has broken the private law unintentionally, at best he has done nothing wrong.

Forfeiture is the main mechanism by which a landlord can terminate a fixed-term lease ahead of time. Most of the other mechanisms for terminating a lease are quite straightforward and unsurprising once the very limited role which the courts have assumed in relation to these matters has been grasped. A fixed-term lease may contain a provision empowering either side to give notice to quit, and the common law would give effect to this, although a tenant may now have some security of tenure in this situation under one of the statutory regimes mentioned above. A lease will also end if a landlord accepts a surrender of the lease from his tenant; and if the tenant buys the reversion on his lease, his leasehold interest and the reversion he buys 'merge' and the independent leasehold interest

112

thereby ends. The difficult question is whether a lease can also terminate through the application of the 'doctrine of frustration'.

The doctrine of frustration is concerned with specifying a set of circumstances in which people can be released from contractual obligations which would otherwise have to be performed. While there is no canonical formula for stating what these circumstances are, the basic idea, which suffices for present purposes, is that where the whole basis upon which the parties made the contract has been destroyed, the doctrine will apply. So people who hired window seats to watch Edward VII's planned coronation procession did not have to pay up when it was postponed because the King was confined to bed. The application of such a doctrine by judges is thus more a matter of delicacy than difficulty. The question is what if any scope does this have for leases?

Any properly drafted lease for any significant duration is likely to provide in advance for the consequences of foreseeable risks. Thus leases commonly contain provisions relating to building insurance, to deal in advance with the problem of fire. Since the allocation of such risks is part of the bargain itself, there is so far as they are concerned no scope for the doctrine of frustration, which rests, in another formulation, on the idea that 'this is not the bargain into which I came'. What, however, about the unforeseeable? If you rent a warehouse for storage purposes, and then the public authorities seal off all access to and from the building so that it is unusable, does rent remain payable?

This brings to the fore the underlying conceptual nature of a leasehold interest and thus warrants closer scrutiny. The obligation, contained in a lease, to pay rent is a contractual obligation of sorts, although failure to pay rent by the tenant gives rise to the additional common law remedy of distress, which enables a landlord to enter and seize a tenant's moveables and sell them in order to recoup rent arrears. Distress is quite independent of the contractual nature of the relationship and is rather rooted in the property relationship between landlord and tenant. The lease is in some sense a 'mix' of contract and conveyance, because the bulk of its contents comprises obligations working out the responsibilities of landlord and tenant respectively, concerning the use and maintenance of the premises let over time, as well as the rent due. But how should this mix be conceptualised?

Property lawyers used to put it in this way. The lease is a conveyance of title, the transfer of a fixed term to the tenant. The covenants contained in this conveyance comprise a set of independent rights and duties made, by the parties, incidental to the term of years. The lease is not one 'bargain' which can be taken as a whole, but an estate in land to which unrelated obligations are attached. This means that a tenant cannot refuse to pay the rent if the landlord defaults on his repair obligations, nor could the landlord set off rent he is owed if the tenant sues him for his default. Each obligation is treated entirely independently. On this view, the only way in which the relationship could end through something analogous to frustration is if the land in which the tenancy exists itself ceases to exist, as where a house on a cliff falls into the sea through erosion. In such an event, all the covenants in the lease would lose their force because there is no longer anything in which either landlord or tenant can have an estate, and therefore no possibility any longer for a landlord-tenant relationship to subsist, no estates to which obligations can be annexed. However, this view has lost its attraction, mainly because it seems 'artificial', and the latest decision on the question[15] holds that a lease is capable of ending through frustration, though this ruling was qualified by saying that in considering whether the doctrine can be invoked in a particular case, all the factors must be weighed, not least the relationship between the frustrating circumstance and the length of the outstanding term. In place of the traditional position that the doctrine 'never' applied to leases was substituted the position that it would 'hardly ever' apply. This formulation has the advantage of flexibility, giving scope to judges to apply the doctrine in a strong case which warrants intervention. It also provides an interesting example of the rather commonplace contemporary judicial reluctance to be bound by what are seen as the shackles of the traditional conceptual repertoire of land law.[16] The main practical difficulties which this approach involves are experienced by law students and their teachers brought up to expect something different from the judges.

Applying the doctrine of frustration to a lease is to treat the lease as a contract. But the lease is a conveyance as well as a contract. It is a title to land, to which obligations can be attached. They commonly originate as promises. But their subsequent enforceability is based on their attachment to a title rather than on the fact that they have

114

been promised. This brings us to the third concern of lawyers. What is the legal effect of the contents of a lease if either landlord or tenant pass on their respective interests?

When a transfer of a fee simple takes place, the transferor may seek, if he is retaining adjacent land, to make some express stipulation with a view to binding the purchaser as to the use in the future to which he may put the land he is buying. To this extent, the courts have been pressured into recognising certain enduring rights and duties between adjacent landowners, and to the extent that this recognition of durability is afforded, these rights are, for lawyers, property rights, and are further explored below. But in the case of the lease, the problem is both slightly different and at the same time more pressing. A lease throws up a problem of adjacency which is not necessarily one of physical proximity. What is adjacent at the core of the landlord-tenant relationship is the conjunction of two estates in land, of the tenant's term of years and the landlord's reversion. And since both may intrinsically endure concurrently over a vast stretch of time, the common law had to formulate a response to the question of the enforceability of leasehold covenants, once either the term or the reversion or both had passed on into new hands, as, in the case of a long lease, was more or less inevitable.

The covenants attached to the term, so far as both sides are concerned, are integral to the relationship which is being created. A tenant's covenants endure throughout the term. The tenant who acquires a lease for ninety years remains liable on his covenants for that term. But since he has acquired what is now recognised by force of statute as an estate in land, he has something of (often considerable) value which can be sold on in the marketplace. If he sells on the term ('assigns' it), will his purchaser (the 'assignee' of the lease) be liable on the covenants he undertook? By the late sixteenth century an affirmative answer was reached by the courts to this question, provided that the covenants in question could be judged to 'touch and concern' the land which was the subject-matter of the lease. The position of new landlords who acquired the reversion of the original lessor had been earlier dealt with by statute in broadly similar terms.

This is nothing to do with contract. Rather, the rights and duties enshrined in the covenants run with the land – or more precisely with the respective estates of landlord and tenant – such that any-one who acquires the estate takes it subject to and with the benefit of all covenants which relate to the land. The original tenant remains liable on his covenants throughout the term because they are his covenants. Statute makes most burdens placed on landlords pass on to their assignees, in this respect overriding the law of contract. Assignees of the reversion thus acquire rights to sue the original tenant on his covenants, even if the new landlord acquired his rights after the original tenant had passed on his interest. By contrast, assignees of the lease are only liable for those breaches of covenant which occur during their time. The position of landlords and tenants over time in respect of leasehold covenants is thus asymmetrical, but the lack of symmetry flows from a combination of the logic of the situation and the intervention of particularistic legislation long ago.

To return briefly to the question of the doctrine of frustration. Since at its core the doctrine is based on the destruction of the substratum of the bargain, it is difficult to see how it is applicable after a lease has been passed on by assignment. One can see how conceptually the doctrine could apply to the tenant's liability on his covenants because his enduring liability, after he has assigned his lease, is based on the fact that they are his covenants and is, in other words, a contractual liability. But the assignee is bound by the covenants which touch and concern the land simply because they are incidental to the estate, the term of years, he acquires in the assign-ment. The only 'bargain' such an assignee enters into, in the normal course of events, is with his assignor before taking the assignment.

PRACTICAL PROBLEMS OF MODERN LEASES

The landlord-tenant relationship, as stated above, has encompassed a wide range of functionally distinct social contexts. This is one reason why special statutory regimes have seemed necessary to cater for the deficiencies left by a largely abstentionist and formalist com-mon law. It is beyond the scope of the present work to discuss these regimes or their deficiencies, which would, in any case, require close examination of the divergent social contexts in which these prob-lems emerge. These regimes, as indicated above, have their own procedures, officials and tribunals to administer them, and in large measure the role of the general courts in respect of them is now confined to particularist questions of statutory interpretation which arise from time to time as to the precise scope of any particular regime.

What can be questioned here is whether it is satisfactory that those social relations whose legal character still rests upon 'general principle', if that it can be called, are adequately dealt with by the present law. We can concentrate on the remaining high ground of common law abstentionism, on that area where the private law of the parties still largely prevails, and raise some questions about whether or not there is a need for either statutory regulation or modification of the common law. This is the area of the long-term lease of residential houses and flats, usually of 99 or 999 years in duration. It is difficult to say in statistical terms how important this area is today, but, if anything, in large conurbations it is of growing significance. We have outlined above areas where in some respects the legal framework of property law seems to be more complicated than is required to meet the needs of ordinary people. This is particularly true of the lease.

1. If you buy a freehold property, you assume that its care and maintenance is up to you. There may be rights and duties which arise in respect of neighbouring property, which we discuss below, but for the most part people's expectations as to the nature of what they are buying, and the legal character of the rights they acquire, coincide. This may not be the case at all with leasehold property, especially leases of parts of buildings under multiple leasehold occupancy. Restrictions on use, allocation of repair obligations between the tenants, even the identity of the present ground rent holder, may all be unknown to a prospective purchaser. All are treated by the estate agents and lawyers involved in the transfer process as technical matters rather than being part and parcel of what is or is not for sale. When the prospective purchaser first puts in his offer, he is commonly forced to do so in ignorance of the precise regime of private law into which he is proposing to buy.

2. The more serious question centres around why it is necessary or preferable for buildings enjoyed in multiple occupancy to be parcelled out as tenancies rather than freeholds. We shall elaborate below on why; for the moment we simply note that it is extremely

difficult as the law stands at present for obligations relating to maintenance or repair of buildings to be directly enforced between freeholders. The general practice of building societies, as a result, is to refuse to lend money to buy 'flying freeholds'. So if a building contains ten flats, the most convenient way from a technical point of view to ensure that each flat owner is obliged, in legal terms, to contribute to the cost of maintaining the building as a whole is by means of leasehold covenants owed to a landlord or freeholder. In this situation, the freeholder is best seen as a purely technical intermediary, inserted for remedial purposes, between the respective tenants. The old function of ground rents has not been lost for a landlord with a sufficient quantity of them, but in many cases the leasehold form is adopted purely because, from the point of view of the enforceability of obligations between tenants, and the ability of prospective purchasers to obtain mortgage finance, it has advantages of a technical kind which lack any extrinsic substantial foundation in the realities of social life. No simple or cast-iron mechanism for embedding such obligations between the tenants themselves is available in English law. And so the combination of an inactive freeholder and a recalcitrant tenant may pose severe obstacles to the maintenance of a building.

The simplest solution to these problems would be to make obligations to do things – like contribute towards the cost of repair – attachable to land so that they were enforceable between freeholders. A less radical solution, though one which would not solve all the difficulties, would be to confer upon tenants the right to buy out the freeholder, as is already the case for leasehold owners of houses.[17]

EQUITABLE LEASES

A lease was, and is, a conveyance of title. So it was, and remains, common for the execution of a lease to be preceded by an agreement, by a contract which sets out the terms of what is to be formalised. If the contract was concluded and then the landowner refused to execute the lease, the best course of action, for someone who could afford it, was to the Chancery, because of the availability of its decree of specific performance. What if the 'lessee' took possession under the contract and before execution of the formal lease? Let us confine the question for the moment to the situation where the contract for the lease was in writing or evidenced by writing. As we shall see, there were particular problems where such a transfer of possession took place on the basis of a purely oral agreement. For present purposes, all that needs to be said is that this problem was short-circuited by the Judicature Acts of the 1870s. If a 'tenant' had taken possession under a contract for a lease, but without the execution under seal of the formal lease for which he had contracted, it ceased to be necessary to await, through the issue of a decree from equity of specific performance of the contract, the physical coming into existence of the lease which had been promised in the contract. In the event of a dispute between any relevant parties, it became possible to ask what the position would be if the contract for a lease had been carried into effect, and to determine the dispute, whatever its nature, as if the lease had been brought into existence along the lines provided for in the contract. In its essentials, an 'equitable lease' is no more than this: a short-circuiting of the adjudicative process effected by the organisational changes of the 1870s in the system of adjudication in England.[18]

MORTGAGES

Lawyers – and bank managers – talk about personal loans and secured loans, and distinguish unsecured from secured creditors. A personal loan is 'just' a contract. The terms of the contract will provide for the terms and time of repayment. If the borrower does not honour these but, say, falls behind with his repayments or fails to repay the lump sum on the due day, the lender's remedies are 'purely' contractual: principally, an action in debt for the sum in question, as happens, for example, today with people who fall seriously into arrears with their credit card repayments.

Where the loan is secured on property, the position is quite different. The lender can still sue for the sum owed as with a personal loan; but, in addition, he has the ability to seek a court order which will enable him to take over the property which serves as security, sell it and take from the proceeds whatever amount is needed to wipe out the debt.

Most people today 'have a mortgage'. They borrow some or all of the money they need to buy a house or flat from a bank or building society and repay the loan over a number of years. The lender secures his loan by means of a mortgage on the property. This transaction is one where, in the normal case, the owner (the 'mortgagor') grants a legal mortgage to the lender (the 'mortgagee'). In the modern law, this arrangement can either take the form of a long lease, or of a 'charge by way of legal mortgage'. This last device, introduced in 1925, is the first time that English law has recognised a conveyancing device which in formal terms is constitutive of the mortgage as a distinctive kind of interest in land. As we will see, this is the main reason why the involvement of the law in mortgages has been so complicated. For most of its history, the mortgage has 'borrowed' from other legal forms. This meant that for centuries, lawyers devoted much energy, especially in the litigation process, to working out criteria for distinguishing what was 'really' a mortgage from what was 'really' something else. Traditionally, the mortgage took the form of a purchase of some sort by the lender of the borrower's land. In formal terms, the mortgagee was, and is, a purchaser, and some of the rules and procedures governing purchasers applied and apply with equal force to lenders on mortgage. Indeed, Cyprian Williams suggested that the investigation of a title by a prospective mortgagee's solicitor should be even more meticulous than in the case of a straightforward conveyance on sale. There were two reasons for this, both of which are still relevant today in certain respects. First, although the mortgage is a type of 'purchase' for English lawyers, it is not usual for a mortgagee to take possession of the mortgaged land from the borrower at the time the loan is made. And so, before 1925, this meant, almost invariably, that since

> . . . a mortgagee . . . gets only a parchment security, and does not, like a [purchaser], enter into possession of the land, there is the more reason for seeing that the evidence of the mortgagor's title is in every respect complete. The title deeds especially should be examined with most particular care; for frauds and forgeries have been far more frequently effected in connection with the mortgage of land, where there is no transfer of actual possession than upon sale (Williams, 1922: 478).

As we shall briefly note, there were exceptions to this, notably what were called 'Welch' mortgages, under which the mortgagee did take possession of the land. But in the standard mortgage – and this remains true today – the mortgagor kept possession of the mortgaged land. In the past, this meant that the borrower continued for the duration of the mortgage to receive the rental income from the land, and in the normal case, pending repayment of the capital advanced by the lender, paid interest on the loan as agreed in the arrangement.

Secondly, in former times:

> purchasers generally buy land with the view of occupying or enjoying it [i.e. taking its rental yield]; they seldom buy it for immediate resale. But the object of a mortgagee is simply to obtain good security for the repayment of his money, whenever he may desire to call it in. . . . While purchasers, therefore, so long as they can obtain a good holding title, are often willing to waive defects of title which will be cured by lapse of time or may be covered by special conditions on a resale, a mortgagee will always desire to get a good marketable title; for he contemplates the possibility of having recourse to a forced sale, when special conditions, in spite of the avidity with which they are usually swallowed at the auction mart, may be depreciatory (Williams, 1922: 477).

Modern mortgages of residential property are somewhat different, in that immediate resale is not envisaged, but only the ability to resell without difficulty should the borrower default. However, as we shall see, lenders on mortgage in the past by no means had their eyes fixed always on resale, and many were content to leave their capital outstanding on mortgage, drawing interest upon it, for very long periods of time. What remains true, in very different conditions, is that those who lend on mortgage are likely, because of the legal advice which they receive, to worry more about possible defects of title, or inconvenient incumbrances upon title, than the purchasers to whom, in the modern world, they advance loans.

Redemption and foreclosure

The modern mortgage with which most people are familiar is different in a number of ways from the more traditional form of mortgage. This legal form has been adapted, from a technical if not a social policy point of view, fairly adequately, to meet modern needs, but the form itself, and the rules which give it expression, were all geared to transactions of a quite different character. We shall start with this.

Mortgage transactions, viewed as a whole, are best regarded as a form of investment, the mortgage device being the mechanism whereby that investment is made secure. This remains true today. The investment or the profit which the lender makes is the interest payable on the capital sum lent. What is different about modern home loans is that their structure is geared fundamentally to repayment of the capital as well as of interest on the capital. This distinguishes it from the traditional use of the mortgage. Once we realize that, we can see how in reality the mortgage device, as employed in the past, was in some ways much closer to an ownership right in a sociological sense than the modern mortgage, and how, given the nature of ownership interests outlined in the previous chapter, the distinction between fragmented ownership and incumbrance on title becomes extremely blurred, as with the lease, but for different reasons. In particular, so long as the paradigm of what land ownership meant was essentially a rental income, the traditional mortgage can be seen as a means of parcelling out the total annual rents, or as a mechanism through which people other than owners of land could participate in its financial fruits. The other side of this comparison between the present and the past is that today we think of the lender as more powerful than the borrower – the ordinary person versus the institutional lender with huge assets and considerable capacity for loss spreading. In the past, by contrast, it was often, although not always, the other way around: the borrower was the person with social and economic power in many transactions; it was the lender, a small person seeking a safe place for his or her capital, who sought through the mortgage device a safe way in which the capital could generate an income over time. The pervasive Victorian literary theme of the beleagured family mortgaged to the brink of ruin was a part, but not the most important part, of the former social and economic reality of mortgaging (cf. Cannadine, 1977; Beckett, 1986).

Land money and equity

For lawyers in the past, there was generally a 'mutuality' in the relationship between mortgagee and mortgagor. In the nature of things, the mortgagor represented 'land' and the mortgagee represented 'money'. Money was for centuries morally suspicious. This was reflected in usury laws, but more fundamentally in a view which saw something dangerous in the shifting, moveable nature of money, in its liquid form and ephemeral mode of functioning. Land, by contrast, was immoveable and constant. The preservation of the status quo, of the established order of society, not surprisingly, seemed to be connected, in an intimate way, with the preservation of the relation between lineage and land, and, less grandly but no less importantly, the maintenance of the security of titles. Here, the courts of equity came to play a crucial role.

A mortgage transaction would commonly identify a particular day upon which the borrower was to repay the capital advanced. Around this date the mutuality of the relationship centred. On the one hand, once this date had passed, the lender was entitled to call for repayment. If at this time the borrower could not repay, the lender could take possession, if the court permitted, of the mortgaged land as absolute owner. This process was known as foreclosure. But the other side of the coin, as the equity courts came to view the matter, was that where the borrower wished to remove the mortgage from his land by repaying the sum advanced, he would be permitted to do so. This was because the equity courts would always compel, except where foreclosure had occurred, the mortgagee to accept repayment in these circumstances as an effective discharge of the mortgage. As a result of this policy of the court, this right became known as the equity of redemption, that is, the right, enforceable in the courts of equity, for a borrower to 'redeem' his mortgaged land from the lender, even after the contractual time for repayment had passed.

But this in turn meant that it was necessary to develop criteria to distinguish a mortgage from a conveyance on sale. In formal terms, mortgagees were purchasers, as we have indicated. Unusually, then, the equity courts, in their desire to protect landowners, were here compelled to address a fundamental distinction between the form and the substance of a transaction prepared by lawyers.

Form and substance of the mortgage

What you find in law books about mortgages in English law is very complicated and more than a little tedious. There are two main reasons for this. The first derives from the traditional nature of the mortgage as such. As a form of carving up rental income, it always made possible, once recognised as a device, the 'pledging' of land as security to more than one mortgagee, up to the total capital value of the land proffered as security, not least because, in the traditional mortgage, the capital advanced on mortgage was commonly much less than the capitalised value of the rental income yielded by the land. (This is one further manifestation of the fact that in the past borrowers were the big men while lenders were the little people.) In other words, it has long been the case that English lawyers needed to develop principles of priority as between mortgagees in the event of disputes arising between them when the debtor/mortgagor defaulted. In analytical terms, a similar question of priorities as between mortgagees arises today against the backdrop of home ownership. But the underlying practical realities of this situation are radically different: these mortgages are less one of many mechanisms for carving up a rental income, much more – almost always – a profit-making device dependent for repayment on the earned income of the borrower, where the possibility of plural mortgaging depends in the end upon permanent inflation in real estate book values.

The second reason for the complexity of the law concerning mortgages, and from a conceptual point of view the more conspicuous, is best grasped in terms of the distinction drawn between form and substance. This is an expression much used by lawyers in the common law world, as much in property law as elsewhere. And, commonly though not exclusively, this distinction, when applied to a legal transaction, can be mapped on to the institutional and jurisdictional distinction between law and equity: common law is 'form', equity is – or 'regards' – 'substance'. But much of the time the drift of this proposition is, at least to modern eyes, not especially profound. It means, for example, that in considering whether an obligation imposed upon someone is genuinely 'negative' or not – as we shall see shortly when restrictive covenants are elaborated – equity asked, whatever form of words was used in the covenant, whether the obligation so created was really negative in nature. So a covenant requiring a building to be used for residential purposes only could be treated as in substance imposing a negative obligation even if it seemed on its surface to be positive: really, such an obligation meant that the covenantee undertook not to use the building for any other purposes. What made the application of the form and substance distinction to mortgages somewhat unusual was that it went well beyond this question (to us rather minor, even if it was not to people of the past) of the meaning of words. In the area of mortgages, it was the meaning of transactions which was at stake in the development of the law by the equity courts, and what is striking about this is the manner in which the courts departed from their conventional stance vis-à-vis the formulaic tradition of the conveyancers.

The legal mortgage of a legal estate took the form of a conveyance of title – whether freehold or leasehold – coupled with a covenant given by the mortgagee to reconvey the title upon repayment ('redemption') of the capital advanced. Against this backdrop, under the banner of looking to the substance of the transaction so created, equity courts asserted a jurisdiction to intervene in favour of the borrower which became known as the equity of redemption.

The basic idea here was that the borrower should always be allowed to redeem if he could repay the loan with interest. In more modern times, it has further been stressed that the borrower's equity here extends to the ability to redeem free of any collateral advantages taken by the mortgagee at the time of the loan. There must be, it is sometimes said, no 'clogs or fetters' on the equity of redemption. This is a rather convoluted way, to modern eyes, of posing directly the question of in what circumstances the courts will give relief against what they consider to be unfair or oppressive transactions.

Why should it follow that where, in substance, a transaction is a mortgage, the borrower must always be able to redeem his land once the legal period for redemption has passed? It is circular to explain this simply in terms of 'equity' or 'justice': equity developed this set of principles because of the way the common law was constrained by the terms of the conveyance and covenant to reconvey, which it simply had to construe and then uphold. The answer might be that English law lacked the clearly defined concept of the hypothec, or rather, such a concept as it came to develop under the label of 'substance' did not, until 1925, with the introduction of the charge by way of legal mortgage, acquire an independent form distinct from the forms used for land transfer, but used the standard forms with some modified covenants. This does in part explain the equity of redemption, since without it the mortgagee in possession of the title deeds could sell on the title, and the mortgagor would be left, at law, with his remedy on the covenant to reconvey. (The equity to redeem is necessary today because the legal redemption period is so short: but this is a conveyancing convention; setting a redemption date at law, as part of the bargain, has been allowed to atrophy because of the equity to redeem. Home purchase mortgages, which are pivotally geared to repayment of capital, have built-in redemption dates though the date may fluctuate during the life of the mortgage.)

This discussion illustrates very sharply a pervasive feature of English property law, and one which accounts for why it so often seems difficult or inaccessible to its students. Instead of simply developing a set of principles, either by statutory regulation or by the casuistry of the common law method, to give assistance in the face of oppressive transactions, lawyers must talk in a complex and convoluted code when addressing quite simple (which is not to say easy-to-answer) questions. Not only do you not need sledgehammers to crack nuts; if you use one, the results can be messy.

Foreclosure and power of sale

As we have indicated, the converse of redemption was, traditionally, foreclosure, through which the lender would gain possession of the mortgaged land. The alternative remedy for a mortgagee was to sell the land under a court order and recoup what was owed from the proceeds of sale, and this is in the normal case the remedy used by modern institutional mortgagees like building societies. When people fall behind on their mortgage repayments, the bank or building society can go to court and in due course repossess the house or flat, put it on the market and recoup its losses from the purchase price. (One might note that in these circumstances, an institutional lender may well provide the finance for the new purchaser, so that in real terms a repossession followed by a sale is, for the lender, a book transfer of the mortgage liability from the defaulting purchaser to the new purchaser.)

There is nothing new about the spectre of foreclosure or repossession haunting a landowner; the burden of debt on the landed estates of the past sometimes became so immense that little if anything from the rent rolls remained after the annual charges had been met, though most great landowners of the past managed to pull back from total ruin (Beckett, 1986: 302–15). Only a few suffered the fate of the second duke of Buckingham, who ended his days in Paddington in the Great Western Hotel (Thompson, 1955).

But because, as we have already seen, mortgage-financed owner-occupation has become the dominant form of tenure in modern England, and because these mortgages are largely financed from earned income, not from rents as in the past, the high levels of unemployment which have been experienced in the 1980s have led in turn to a significant increase in the volume of mortgage defaults, and have thus hooked up to the more general problem of homelessness. Whether or not the present procedures which regulate the processing of repossession claims by mortgagees through the courts are adequate cannot be elaborated upon here; but the 'right to buy' policies of Mrs Thatcher's administrations mean that what for lawyers is a relatively prosaic element of the judicial process is likely to assume a sharpened significance for a widening section of the population.

6

Land Use and Land Obligations

Lawyers have also been required to invent devices for the exploitation and restriction of the use value of land. Not surprisingly, given the well 'planned' character of Roman, and especially Graeco-Roman cities, precedents for such conceptualisation already existed in Roman law. Predictably, what most interested medieval lawyers – and what was most elaborated by Roman jurists – were what we would call 'private' mechanisms for controlling land use. Medieval lawyers had two principal ways at their disposal of doing things: grants of use rights and promises as to use, which became easements and profits on the one hand, and covenants on the other.

On the one hand, lawyers came to recognize, by analogy with the process of 'granting' estates in land, the grant of ancillary rights of use known as 'easements', to benefit the enjoyment of land (both agricultural and urban), such that these benefits (and their correlative burdens) could be attached to the land and so 'run' with it, i.e. benefit and bind successors in title. The content of such rights of use of land belonging to another was principally bounded by the limit that such rights should not involve the expenditure of money. By contrast with mortgages, so far as land obligations were concerned, the courts stopped at permitting heirs to be burdened for the future with expensive charges. 'Covenants', solemn promises to do things or not to do things, were a different matter. If the performance of a promise cost money, it cost the money of the person making the promise. The benefit of such promises could be allowed to run with land – to 'enure' to the benefit of successors in title to the original person taking the promise – but the obligation was not so permitted to run. We have already seen that the position was for a long time different with leasehold covenants. Here the courts were willing to enforce covenants contained in leases beyond the original parties provided that they benefited the land which was the subject-matter of the lease. In the nineteenth century, equity came to afford similar recognition of negative covenants restricting land use between freeholders.

To summarise: in practical terms, these rights take two main forms. Some enable one landowner to enter the land of another and do things on that land – such as walk across it or hang a sign on it or store goods on it – even though that land does not, by definition, belong to him. The other main type of right takes the form of enabling the person with the right to require the landowner subject to it either to do things on the subjected land or to refrain from doing things on that land, either of which will benefit the holder of the right in his enjoyment of his land. Examples include the obligation to maintain hedges and ditches, or to refrain from using agricultural or residential land for commercial or industrial purposes.

Broadly, the first category of rights take the form of easements, and the second covenants. Both types of rights can, with less ambivalence than was the case with the lease or the mortgage, be regarded as ancillary to ownership rights, or, for land transfer purposes, as incumbrances upon title rather than as fragments of title. Insofar as this distinction can be given a clear meaning, we might say that these 'subsidiary' rights which we now examine are for the most part – again there are exceptions – rights which possess the quality of durability through time but lack the quality of independent transmissibility. These are rights, in other words, which are transmissible in a limited way, but are only recognised if attached or annexed to a freely transmissible interest like a lease or a fee simple. They are rights which cannot be detached from the title to which they are ancillary and the enjoyment of which they benefit or enhance (though they may be exercisable too by those with derivative titles). They are rights which cannot be transferred in their own right but only in the course of the transfer of something else which, in principle, can.

EASEMENTS

As we noted in the previous chapter, distinctions which are meaningful for lawyers are not always observable in the brute facts (if they can be so described) of everyday life. If one farmer lets his neighbour drive his cattle across one of his fields, lawyers can conceptualise the arrangement or transaction as involving the grant of an easement, or as a mere licence. An observer, however, may have no idea at all, merely looking on, whether the relationship in legal terms between such farmers is one involving property rights or not, since whatever the nature of the legal relationship, the mode of use may be the same, equally intensive or equally sporadic.

Lawyers distinguish easements from ownership rights on the one hand and from personal rights on the other. Easements differ from ownership rights both in their scope and in the extent to which they are transmissible. Ownership rights involve the right to possession of the land (though as we have seen, there are many ways in which the right to possession can be postponed, as in the reversion on a lease). It is usually said of easements that they must not be so comprehensive: an easement cannot amount to conferring exclusive possession of the land over which the easement is claimed. An easement enables one landowner to tap the resources of an adjacent owner, to make limited use of land belonging to another. Sometimes this distinction between easement and ownership is clear-cut. If one farmer has a right of way over the land of a neighbour, he may from time to time drive his cattle across the neighbour's land, but otherwise the neighbour's freedom to use his land fully is unimpaired. But in the case of easements of storage, the limitations upon the owner's freedom may be more extensive. If one farmer has the right to store sacks of corn in a neighbour's barn, the owner of the barn can hardly be said to 'enjoy' it while it contains the other farmer's sacks. In a case of this kind, it is not obvious where ownership ends and easement begins.

Easements are also transmissible in a sense much more limited than ownership rights are. They are ancillary to, or 'annexed' to, title; they run with the land. This means that the owner of a field may sell it or give it away to anyone he chooses. Easements are transferrable only to the person to whom ownership is transferred. Easements are property rights because of their (limited) transmissibility and because they can endure against successive owners of the land over which they are held. In both respects they differ from licences. Licences are 'personal' in two senses: the rights they confer may be enjoyed only by those to whom they are granted, and they bind only those who grant them.

These rights are sometimes called 'servitudes', after Roman law, indicating that the core idea is the subjection of one land ownership to another. The land on which the obligation is imposed is called the 'servient tenement' and the land which derives the benefit is the 'dominant tenement'. The more ponderous term used more commonly by English lawyers to describe such interests is 'incorporeal hereditament'. This emphasises the nature of the right rather than the obligation. Obviously, though, the two are correlative, since we are here dealing with property rights which take the form of attaching rights in the one case and obligations in the other to titles to land, rights which, for lawyers, are property rights precisely because they are attached to titles and possess, for the most part, the same durability as the title to which they are attached.

As we have noted, most easements involve a right to do something on land belonging to another without taking any of the produce of that land, while covenants impose obligations upon the owner of land subjected to the covenant to do or refrain from doing something on his own land. But this neat distinction itself disintegrates when we examine certain rights which have been recognised as easements. Certain rights which lawyers have long treated as easements function more like covenants insofar as they involve restraining action by the servient owner on his land rather than conferring active benefits upon the owner of the land to which the easement is attached. Examples of this are easements which prevent the disruption of the flow of light or air to premises, which confer a right of support for buildings on one piece of land from soil or buildings on adjacent land, and rights which restrain a landowner from interfering with an established flow of water through his land to the land of another.

The difficulty which we here encounter of drawing clear – or tidy – conceptual boundaries once again results from the imprint of the past upon the present. Many rights still today recognised as easements – for example, rights of way, light and water – have been recognised since medieval times for the simple reason that the functional pressures for their continued recognition have operated for centuries and not ceased to exist, pressures which flow, indeed, from some very elementary and long-lasting aspects of the spatial organisation of settled social life. In this respect, negative easements, which restrict the activities or scope of the servient owner rather than enabling or enhancing the capacities of dominant owners, are best seen as an early response to basic problems which arise in situations where the enjoyment of one plot of land or building is intrinsically affected by the activity of the owner of the adjacent land. And the antiquity of easements is reflected in the way lawyers talk about their creation even today. They are said to be created by 'grant' or 'reservation', and one means of asserting a prescriptive right is by 'lost modern grant'. The kind of right which is capable of being an easement, it is said, must 'lie in grant'.

All this, while no doubt analytically 'sound', can make the study of easements rather obscure. In practical terms, in the modern and not so modern world, easements come into existence in two essentially different ways. First, where part of a block of land is sold off, vendor and purchaser may expressly direct their minds (or their lawyers may direct them) to the question whether, after the sale, either side should obtain any easements – say rights of way – over the land retained or acquired by the other. Secondly, even where the parties' minds are not expressly directed to the question, so that nothing is written down in formal language in the transfer of title to the plot being sold, a dispute may subsequently come before the courts, and the court will have to decide whether an easement should be implied into the transfer of title, as part of the bargain, in favour of the former vendor or purchaser. Both of these matters are best regarded, for the most part, as pertaining to the business of the management of land transfer and the adjudication of disputes consequent upon the management of land transfer by lawyers.

The second complex of problems which have presented themselves to lawyers spring from life – or the social organisation of land use – rather than law. This is the acquisition of easements by prescription, which essentially means that a landowner should be entitled to continue to do something on a neighbour's land just because he has in fact done it for a very long time. This is another case of clothing fact – what just happens – with 'right'. No legal system can ignore the problem of prescriptive rights and their 'acquisition', but the extraordinary complexity of English law in this area suggests considerable discomfort with the whole idea.

PROFITS

Most of the law books discuss alongside easements a category of 'use rights' called 'profits'. A profit gives its holder the right to take something from land belonging to another: to dig clay or cut turf, to pasture animals, to catch fish and game, to mine for coal or extract oil. These are commonly treated as servitudes, and share, with easements, the characteristic that whatever the content of your right, it involves – subject to some exceptions regarding easements introduced below – your entering upon land belonging to another in order to perform some operation there. There, however, the common characteristics stop, since the profit can better be regarded as another legal mechanism for carving up the fruits of the land.

This distinctive feature of the profit was long recognised by lawyers insofar as they allowed the profit, but not the easement, to exist 'in gross', that is, to operate as a property right even though its holder had no land of his own to which the right was attached. Obviously, profits could be annexed to land and through so doing make that land more valuable; but there has long been no requirement that recognition of a profit as a property right should depend upon such annexation to a title taking place. The fact that such rights could be annexed may be one reason why profits have tended to be classified alongside easements – or subsidiary rights – rather than being incorporated into the analysis of how title to land can be fragmented. But perhaps there is another reason for the classificatory difficulty. Easements and profits are both ways of fashioning rights relating to the physical use of land. When we talk about 'the use and enjoyment' of land, two different things may be meant: its monetary yield, that is, the rental income it is capable of generating; or its enjoyment in physical terms, whether this means walking across it or picking the fruit or cutting the timber growing on it. English lawyers drew a fairly sharp division between the two, the first underpinning their analysis of title, the second their analysis of servitudes. To refer again to the metaphysics of the common law, a profit was a right to the substance of the land, as in a right to take minerals; as we have seen, a rent was a right to what the substance could be made to yield. Of course, as always, there were exceptions. Thus Bullen observes: 'In the case of mines . . . it seems that a rent may consist of a portion of the ore, which is the substance of the land itself' (1899: 20n.a).

COVENANTS

Covenants restricting the way in which a landowner can use his land are more recent in origin. That they have emerged as a separate type of property right or servitude can be explained in fairly simple terms. The way lawyers conceptualised easements reflects a social context in which the capacity to confer ancillary benefits annexed to titles to land could increase the value of a particular estate, but, for the most part, except so far as securing flows of light and water were concerned, it did not seem necessary to enshrine in the form of a property right what a landowner could do with his land. The courts might and did come under pressure to provide remedial assistance where a landowner's use of his land was particularly noxious or unpleasant to his neighbours; hence that branch of the law of tort called nuisance. But in the past, standards of tolerance were higher and the technological capacity to cause disturbance more limited. The layout of most medieval towns suggests no great concern with prospect or amenity. 'Merrie England' was a country of filth, fire and stench.

Nonetheless, for reasons which cannot be developed here, by the eighteenth century social values seem to have changed, and a certain ruralisation of urban as well as rural England seems to have occurred. Lawyers first gave expression to this in terms of the kinds of covenants they inserted in, for example, building leases. In due course, however, they endeavoured to insert similar covenants in conveyances of freehold, where no continuing landlord-tenant relationship could support the obligation created by the covenant once the title had passed out of the hands of the original covenantor.

Covenants are property rights to the extent that, although they originate in agreement between individual landowners, and as such are enforceable as contracts by the original parties, they are treated as attached, by analogy with easements, to the dominant and servient tenements concerned. Again by analogy with easements, they are not recognised as capable of being so attached unless this proximate relationship of benefit and burden can be shown. But this applies only where the content of the covenant undertaken by a landowner is negative in character, where, in other words, no positive action is required of him. Covenants which impose positive obligations – to maintain a fence or wall or to dig a ditch – have always been treated differently. The benefit of such covenants, it has long been recognised, can attach to the land so that the right to enforce them will 'run' automatically with the land. (Whether it does or not is for the parties to decide when the covenant is made.) But the obligation so created cannot be attached to the land of the covenantor; it remains personal to him and will become unenforceable when his title passes on or he becomes unobtainable. This has an important practical consequence today, concerning especially whether the obligation to maintain or repair buildings can be made to run with land. The lease was and, at the time of writing, remains the only secure way positive obligations could be attached to titles to land.[19] And such obligations are important, as between neighbours, where they share common structural elements of a building – the foundations, the roof – as is the case in flats and tenements. A flat developer today gets his basic return by selling leases of the flats he has developed. He must sell them as leases because the purchasers will not be able to raise mortgage finance if he sells the flats as freeholds. And the purchasers will not get such finance because as things stand at the time of writing positive covenants relating, for example, to repair, cannot be enforced between freeholders, and therefore freehold flats are considered to provide poor security by institutional lenders. In other words, today, the 'lease' is used as a form which has been disengaged from the substance of the transaction. Leases of this sort have become the vehicle of a new kind of practice, the service charge of the freeholder of a building converted into flats by way of leases containing positive covenants relating to repair and maintenance. The brute fact is that the lessees – the owners of the flats – must pay the costs of maintenance and repair. But if a lease places the responsibility for carrying out the work upon the lessor (whether it does or not is largely up to the initial developer), there is a risk that the lessor may charge almost regardless of the service he provides. Statute now gives lessees of flats the right to go to court if these charges are unreasonable (Landlord and Tenant Act 1985). An alternative approach would be to change the old rules and enable positive obligations to be attached to freeholds. This would have the added advantage of making it possible to simplify the esoteric form in which the ownership of units in multiple dwellings is organised today.

Because restrictive covenants were enforced by the courts of equity, their enforceability against a landowner depended upon the doctrine of notice, and a purchaser without notice of a covenant binding his land took free from it. Various procedures for the registration of such covenants were introduced in 1925, and are outlined in a later chapter. It can be noted at this stage, though, that the books rightly insist that in deciding whether a particular covenant is enforceable as a land obligation, you must, once beyond privity of contract, ask whether the benefit has passed to the plaintiff and the burden to the defendant as two independent questions. This might suggest that there is a symmetrical relation between the two sides. But there is not exactly. There is one question relating to both benefit and burden: whether, in each case, it 'passes', which is part of the body of learning concerning land transfer and the appropriate conveyancing procedures. A second question arises with the benefit alone: 'does this claimed right "in fact" benefit the plaintiff's land or title?' This is a question which operates at a quite different level.

In previous chapters we have considered how the past grips the present in the way English land law is put together and how this makes many matters more convoluted or oblique than seems necessary. Questions which could be put directly are put indirectly, or have to be considered in a curious, obscure code. The same is true with land obligations. But perhaps because the questions here are not just questions for conveyancers, that is, questions of form or of mechanics, but also questions of substance, some of the fundamental distinctions in this area have been discredited. In particular, the Law Commission has now proposed that positive and negative covenants should be assimilated. The old metaphysics of the common law have lost their appeal for the modern mind.

PUBLIC CONTROL OF LAND USE

The use of covenants in building leases and in schemes of development marked a further extension of the private regulation of land use. To the extent that these devices were upheld and enforced by the courts, they constituted a private law which governed and governs the use of land by its owners. Limited inroads have been made upon this practice. In particular, legislation now empowers the Lands Tribunal to set aside restrictive covenants which have become obsolete.

More generally, the whole system of 'private' control of land use now exists in parallel with a public system of control. For centuries, public control of the use of land took the form of prohibition: the issue of regulations forbidding anyone to erect a building more than such and such a height and so on. In the twentieth century, public control has assumed a more positive role.

Here it is necessary to distinguish two processes: public control of land development, and forward planning of land development by public authorities. Public control of land use aims at maximising the sum total of land values by minimising the costs and negative side-effects of the intensification of land use. This is done essentially by requiring individual landowners who wish to carry out certain operations on their land, or change its use, even if the land is subject to no privately imposed restrictions, to seek planning permission from the local authority for such change of use.

Since the Second World War in particular, following the mass destruction of many urban areas through bombing, a range of attempts has been made to 'plan' how land is used. Local authorities have been required to produce plans for the general nature of development in their areas, which, in turn, have been supervised or overseen by the central departments of state.

Control of land use by public authorities does not require plans, though the existence of plans may make the decision-making process on particular applications seem less arbitrary. If plans for cities, counties or regions exist, then decision-making on particular proposed changes of use can be made with reference to such plans, and equally, the formulation of proposals for development by private individuals or companies can use the plan as a point of reference for predicting the likely success of their proposal (since the formulation of proposals costs time and money). It is largely with reference to this broad objective of planning that local authorities have been empowered to compel private owners to sell to them land required for development.

The history of the planning system is largely caught up in the history of the land development industry on the one hand and the history of central and local government relations on the other, and lies beyond our scope here. Given the nature of modern life, and the very considerable side-effects which uncontrolled development can generate – especially in the area of transportation – it is generally accepted that public control is inevitable and necessary. But coherent planning has been less successful, and whether local authorities will continue to be required to plan in any serious sense is now in question. Private regulation of land use, by contrast, remains of great importance in a practical sense, and the recent suggestion of the Law Commission that positive covenants should run with the land in the same way as restrictive covenants, if adopted, would extend even further the importance of the 'private law' of land.

7

Transfer and the Circulation of Things

After the sharing of food, the transfer of the possessions of someone who has died, few though these might be, to those who still remain has, in most societies, to be resolved. The Pharaonic solution in which your things go with your body to the tomb, and the destruction of your things along with your body, are both relatively rare in human experience.

Death is, however, only one moment in the developmental cycle, and the circulation of possessions is more widely associated with what are decisive moments in this cycle in many societies, especially birth and marriage as well as death. Two principal ways of making sense of this fact are, first, a functional and, secondly, a semiological explanation. In the first, the circulation of things, often linked, as with marriage, to the circulation of people (e.g. bridewealth and dowry), is understood as an integrative mechanism, as social cement. One objection to this view is that norms relating to the exchange of things at key points in the developmental cycle are as generative of conflict as of social peace. The semiological approach sees exchange as signifying, as marking an event. People communicate with each other through the exchange of things. Mauss says that men could pledge their honour before they could sign their names (1925; tr. 1966, 1969:36), and quickly adds that they often used things as 'pledges'. The circulation of things could symbolize or represent the movement of honour within a social group.

Moreover, in any society, many acts of exchange, through which things circulate between people, take place quite independently of the developmental cycle, as immediate responses to the needs of the moment. But the inner logic of exchange – what it 'means' to the members of the group – is not necessarily 'economic', if by this we mean that 'an economy comprises a separate sphere of instrumental or practical action' such that economic analysis '. . . can be used to

139

analyse patterns of livelihood everywhere' (Gudeman, 1986:vii). Within such an economic perspective, exchange is understood as a further instrumental or practical act, a primordial mutual act in which 'barter' is treated as an early form of sale, in which exchange involves the reciprocal transfer of a material capability, enabling each party to the transaction to satisfy, directly or indirectly, his material needs. In this perspective, it is the satisfaction of these needs which serves to motivate the exchange. Economists would no doubt readily admit that other, 'extraneous', elements may be visible in the transactions of 'real life': there may be elements which motivate exchange – as in the choice of trading partner – which are not readily attributable to the purely practical objective of the satisfaction of material needs. The main function or objective (obviously the two are not the same) of trading with particular partners may be to cement an alliance with them. This may be the indigenous explanation for the object of the exercise, or the interpretation placed upon the exchange by an anthropologist who observes it. In either case, there are ways of seeing the exchange which diverge sharply from the model of economic rationality which we largely take for granted in the West. Where this leads is a matter of immense difficulty and quite beyond our scope. But it is not just that Other Cultures are different; their study may also alert us to aspects of our own experience which we leave unstated.

These 'non-rational' elements are more readily discerned in the way in which we think about 'gift', which, as we shall see, lawyers, in contrast to many social scientists, do not treat as a form of exchange at all but as its opposite. The transmission of material capability – of the capacity to satisfy material needs through the consumption of things – is clearly a feature of many gift exchanges, as with many practices of inheritance (for which, see Chapter 2 above). But in our understanding of gift, other, additional, 'meanings' are often at work. Wedding presents transfer material capability, but also cement relations between groups and mark important changes of status for the partners to the marriage. The functional and semiological aspects of the transaction are relatively visible. Sometimes, indeed, it is mainly the semiological element which renders the gift intelligible, as where the 'largest' share in the family property passes to the eldest son by virtue of his position in the family but where such transmission confers no substantial material capability (the ancestral watch or one more goat than the younger brothers and/or sisters). Here, the principal role of the gift is to mark who he is.

In general terms, the economic understanding of the circulation of things provides limited, and often parochial, purchase on this central facet of human experience. As Mauss suggested many years ago, people communicate with each other in a complex variety of ways when they handle, exchange or destroy things. Honour and shame, political superiority and subordination, alliance and separation, maintenance and change of status: one or more of these can be at stake when things circulate between people as well as or in place of the transfer of the ability to satisfy material needs in which the economist would ground the logic of exchange.

Nor does exchange, even today, require lawyers or courts: trade without rulers is a common enough feature of social experience (see, for example, Northrup, 1978). It is the coming of literacy, more than anything, which enables lawyers to get their hands on the business of exchange. This comes about in two ways. First, and most important, lawyers come upon the scene as writers, recording in writing the fact of transfer, and, in the process, developing a special language for the act of recording, until a point is reached where the writing ceases to be a mere record of an act and becomes constitutive of the act itself. Secondly, presupposing such developments, lawyers become readers of such writing, when the writing is scrutinized for proof of title, or by a judge in a dispute which is taken to court. We see in this chapter that the use of writing developed with particular intensity in relation to the circulation of titles to land. This has had the result that English land law is very largely the product of a dialectic between the work of lawyers as writers and lawyers as readers. The complexity of land law is largely attributable to the fact that lawyers have long been so good with words.

LAWYERS AND TRANSFER MANAGEMENT

Moveables

Most moveables by definition are easy to transfer and circulate within a society with only minimal involvement on the part of lawyers. As already indicated, this is one reason why English conceptions of personal property are relatively undeveloped, and geared primarily to a system of remedies for the recovery of chattels or their value through the legal process. But, as we have seen, English lawyers distinguish property from the thing itself. This opens up the possibility that transfer of title will occur at a different time from transfer of the thing to which the title relates. In examining transfer in English law, we are looking at (i) lawyers' recognition of the facts of life (clothing fact with right again: delivery as effecting a transfer of title); (ii) lawyers' development of artificial mechanisms for transferring title (notably deeds); (iii) lawyers' specification of rules designed to determine in any particular case the moment in time when title passes. This third aspect is of particular importance in the context of buying and selling, and can conveniently be treated first.

(a) SALE

Selling is a social process which can be privately arranged between two individuals, and this is what is meant, today, by the phrase 'sale by private treaty'. In the modern world, we take this process of buying and selling for granted, since there are so many means of communication through which selling can occur. But in many societies, this is precisely the difficulty: establishing contact in the first place between buyer and seller. In this context the phenomenon of the market, whether permanent, as in the bazaar or souk, or periodic, as in the market in the English country town, is the commonest form of organising exchange through sale. Transacting by private treaty still provides the model for the management by lawyers of the sale of land. The market, where exchange is rapid and many matters have to be taken on trust, provides the model for how lawyers think about the sale of other things.

In English law, transfer of title by sale has two main ingredients. First, an agreement between buyer and seller. Secondly, a quid pro quo – you get the car and I get the money. This is what lawyers call 'consideration'. This second element is conventionally taken to distinguish sale from gift; we return below to this distinction. Unlike land, agreements for the sale of moveables need no formality to be effective in law. Indeed, nothing need even be said: you pay your money and take the thing away. The 'agreement' is inferred from the conduct of the parties. Witnesses are not required. Written agreements or written evidence (e.g. a receipt) of the transaction will be of decisive importance if there is later a dispute, but legally they are 'optional extras'.

So much for 'agreement'. The second question is when does title pass? If you decide to sell your car, when does your title to the car pass to the buyer? Perhaps the most obvious answer is that title passes when he takes the keys and registration book from you and drives away. But what if the buyer puts down a deposit? Even in the everyday world, people might be unsure about the question of title at that point. In fact, there are several other possibilities. Title might pass as soon as you reach agreement and shake hands on the deal. It might pass when the money is paid. It might pass at a time which the two of you agree it should.

Behind the question of time is the question of risk. Cars are dangerous and vulnerable things, easy to steal and easy to destroy. Cars are risky; insurance provides a mechanism for anticipating risk. Buyer and seller need to know about when title passes so that they know when the risk passes from one to the other, and thus who must insure what, and when.

Some civil law jurisdictions have a simple rule about the passing of title. It passes when the thing is delivered by the seller into the hands of the buyer. No doubt this seems sensible to many people. If you buy a guard dog, you would probably assume that it becomes yours from the time when you take it away, because from that time you have to feed it, make sure it does not maul innocent people, in short, become responsible for it. But English law treats the intention of the parties as decisive. The Sale of Goods Act 1893 provides that title under a contract of sale passes 'when the contracting parties intend it to pass'. If there is no discernible intention, title passes at the time the contract is made.

The essential elements of a transfer of title by sale, are, then, agreement and consideration. But what else, if anything, should concern a buyer who seeks to obtain a good title to moveable things? How far is he concerned with titles 'earlier' than that of the seller? We have already seen that the general rule here is that the seller cannot pass on a better title than he himself has (*nemo dat quod non habet*). From this it follows that the buyer is at risk if titles superior to that of the seller lurk in the background. In this context, there are some exceptions to *nemo dat* which can now be introduced.

One way of looking at the *nemo dat* principle is to treat it as protecting the integrity of title, as ensuring that someone with a 'good' title does not lose it to someone who comes later upon the thing. So the more rigidly *nemo dat* is applied, the more pressure there is on a buyer to investigate the quality of the title on offer. Here too English lawyers have distinguished land from other things. Title to land requires thorough investigation; the law is more accommodating when it comes to other things. The primary responsibility placed upon a buyer in a 'commercial' rather than land transaction is that he act in good faith. Beyond that are some specific exceptions to *nemo dat* where an innocent purchaser of moveable objects will be able to defend himself against a claimant with 'good' title.

1. If you hand something over to an agent so that he can sell it for you, the agent can pass a good title to a purchaser even though title remains with you, provided he was given the thing as an agent to sell it. So if a dealer sells your car while it is in his hands to be repaired, title does not pass to the buyer under this exception.

2. If the seller lets the buyer take possession of the thing before title has passed, the buyer can pass a good title to an innocent purchaser even though he himself does not yet have title.

3. Conversely, if the seller remains in possession after title has passed to the buyer under the contract of sale, a third party can acquire good title from the seller.

The rationale of these exceptions to *nemo dat* is fairly obvious. The innocent purchaser in whose favour these exceptions are made is less able to protect himself than the person who would succeed if *nemo dat* was strictly applied. If you sell through an agent, you should choose an honest one. If you are selling, you should hold on to the thing until you have been paid. If you are buying, you should take control of the thing once you have paid the price. The law assumes that such practical rules govern transactions in the marketplace.

Underpinning these exceptions is the more basic fact that titles in commercial transactions are commonly lacking in documentary support, and it is this, as we shall shortly see, which sharply distinguishes transfers of title to land in the English system. Put differently, there has always been pressure in the direction of enabling buyers to assume that those who have moveable things own them, at least if there is nothing clandestine about it. This is manifested clearly in the oldest exception to *nemo dat*, which can be traced back to the Middle Ages.

4. Anyone who buys in 'market overt' acquires secure title to the thing he buys. 'Market' means those open-air and street markets which are 'legally constituted' by local laws or long established custom at familiar sites and times. This exception to *nemo dat* is different from the three already mentioned in one crucial respect. The first three are all premised upon the person with the original title entering into a commercial transaction in the first place. As we have indicated, those exceptions are based on a set of assumptions about how those who trade should look after their own interests. The market overt exception, by contrast, works to defeat title even where the original owner is wholly innocent – the victim, for example, of theft.

(b) GIFT

As we have said, lawyers distinguish sharply between sale and gift, both in terms of their respective natures and in the legal consequences which attach to each. More precisely: lawyers classify promises into two distinct categories, using the presence or absence of consideration as the yardstick. Gratuitous promises, one-sided 'unilateral' promises where I give you my promise – my word – but receive nothing in return, are unenforceable in law. But where promises are exchanged – where I give you my promise in return for your promise – the law will enforce each side of the bargain. If the promise relates to a transfer of title to a thing, the gratuitous promise does nothing at all in legal terms, whereas, as seen above, the mere exchange of promises is capable of passing title in law.

Lawyers look upon gift as at core a unilateral transaction, by contrast with the bilateral character of sale. Gift is not treated as a mode of exchange. In this respect, the legal definition of gift differs sometimes quite sharply from the social meaning of gift in many cultures, including, perhaps, our own.

In some societies, giving 'buys' you prestige. As Mauss put it:

> Between vassals and chiefs, between vassals and their henchmen, the hierarchy is established by means of . . . gifts. To give is to show one's superiority, to show that one is something more and higher, that one is *magister*. To accept without returning or

repaying more is to face subordination, to become a client and subservient, to become minister (1925; tr. 1966, 1969:72).

Moreover, as Bourdieu has observed, in many societies gifts generate the obligation to give back. But such obligations are scripted in a complex way:

> In every society it may be observed that, if it is not to constitute an insult, the counter-gift must be deferred and different, because the immediate return of an exactly identical object clearly amounts to a refusal (i.e. the return of the same object). Thus gift exchange is opposed on the one hand to swapping, which . . . telescopes gift and counter-gift into the same instant, and on the other hand, to lending, in which the return of the loan is explicitly guaranteed by a juridical act and is thus already accomplished at the very moment of the drawing up of a contract capable of ensuring that the acts it prescribes are predictable and calculable (1972; tr. 1977:5, italics removed).

Lawyers' involvement in giving arises in three contexts. First, the devising of mechanisms for giving which will be enforceable in courts. Secondly, the development of categories to conceptualise in legal terms what people do with their things in the course of ordinary life; thirdly, the formulation of rules (beyond our present scope) to limit the effects of the general rules if people, in giving, harm others, notably their creditors.

(i) Legal artifice

The courts will only enforce a gratuitous promise to transfer a thing if the promise is formally written down in a deed of gift. A deed is a written 'instrument' (a stylised mechanism for achieving a result) signed and sealed by the person making the gift and then 'delivered'. 'Delivery' is a ceremonial act which is accomplished when the donor places his hand on the seal and says: 'I deliver this as my act and deed.' In practical terms, such a deed functions to provide evidentiary support for the fact that a gift took place by actual delivery. However its legal effect is the same whether or not the thing or the deed is handed over after the solemn declaration of delivery. And the desire to provide enduring evidentiary support for gratuitous transfers seems to be how this piece of legal artifice arose in the first place (Clanchy, 1979).

The deed itself is, then, the instrument which effects transfer of title by way of gift. But it stylises a more primordial – and still more common – mode of giving, namely, the simple physical act whereby one person hands a thing over to another. The deed, one might say, has a representational character; it 'stands for', substitutes for, but equally is premised upon, the act of giving itself.

(ii) Delivery

The transfer of title by actual, physical, delivery of the thing is not in its essentials a piece of legal artifice. Rather, it is something which happens in the social world, of which lawyers have to make sense. That is, it is a mode of social behaviour which lawyers had to draw in to their own conceptual scheme. Here, then, the rule is drawn from the social world: 'Title passes with delivery.' Lawyers conceptualised delivery, the physical act, as the instrument for passing title, and equally treated the act of delivery as proving or establishing, in evidential terms, that a transfer of title had taken place.

Given that transfer by deed is a piece of legal artifice, it posed only mechanical problems for lawyers, principally to do with verbal formulae. But since delivery represents a legal conceptualisation of what people simply did and do, it inevitably throws up a range of problems concerning what the legal concept of delivery exactly means.

Actual physical transfer of a thing is simple enough. But some things may be so big or heavy that they cannot simply be picked up by me and handed to you. Further, if I want to give you a set or collection of things, do I have to hand over each individual item of the set for the law to recognize the transfer as valid? Yet again, I may not have the thing I wish to give you immediately to hand; it may be out on loan or buried among my mess. Must I get it back or find it before I can give it to you? You might even have the thing I want to give you already in your possession, because you hired it or borrowed it, or are taking care of it for me. Must you return it to me before I can give it to you? Such routine questions required lawyers to stylize their conception of delivery itself. First, large heavy things could be transferred by 'symbolical delivery'. Delivery will be taken to have occurred by lawyers if, for example, the donor places his hand upon the thing and declares that he gives it to the donee, or if he hands over his receipt (from when he bought it) or some other document relating to the thing. If someone else has the thing at the moment, say on loan or hire, the donor can pass title to you by telling that person of the gift and getting him to acknowledge that it now belongs to you. If the donor cannot find the thing but tells you where he thinks it might be, it will be yours if and when you find it. And words of gift suffice if the donee already has the thing at the time the donor wants to make the gift. In the case of sets or collections of things, however, each item must be handed over. I cannot give you my entire dinner service by handing over the sauceboat to you. If that is all I do, then that is all you get in law.

A gift cannot be forced upon someone. To this limited extent, although the law regards gift as a non-reciprocal relationship, it involves an element of consent. The donee can refuse the gift. It follows that where the donee is ignorant of the gift at the time that it is made – most obviously, in such a situation, where it is made by deed – he can, on discovery of the gift, repudiate it. In such perhaps rather unlikely circumstances, the legal position is not clear. Does title pass provisionally to the donee at the time of the gift and then revert to the donor on repudiation? Or does title remain with the donor until the gift is accepted by the donee? Or does a repudiated gift mean that title to the thing becomes vacant following the repudiation? We do not know the answers to these questions. As so often in English law, this may be because no practical pressures lead to them being asked in the first place.

(iii) Equitable modification: the resulting trust

An equitable device which we outlined above must be reintroduced at this stage. Outside the highly stylised context of the deed of gift, where legal titles change hands, the meaning of the transaction may be ambiguous to lawyers and require interpretation. In legal terms, it may be quite clear that a sale, and the resultant passing of title, has taken place. But a need for interpretation may arise in terms of the position of the buyer vis-à-vis the legal title he has acquired. If someone else put up the money, the courts of equity have long exercised a jurisdiction to impose a trust upon the buyer. They do this where there is no evidence of loan or gift from the provider of the money to the buyer. A trust is presumed in such circumstances, unless a counter-presumption of gift (the presumption of advancement, rooted in the grid of pre-mortem inheritance – see above) is brought into play by the facts of the case.

Assignment of choses in action

Intangible things present problems of transfer which are absent in the case of tangible things. First, and most obviously, there is no physical thing to circulate, nothing to be delivered or received. Intangible things, as creatures of the law in the first place, require legal artifice for their transfer. Secondly, the transfer of title to some intangibles involves third parties in a way that is often not the case with moveables or land. Debt provides an example. Its transfer essentially involves ensuring that the debtor will pay the assignee of the debt. In their very nature, transfers of rights of this kind affect third parties as well as transferor and transferee.

Section 136 of the Law of Property Act 1925 provides a general set of formalities for transferring title to debts, which applies to both sales and gifts. It requires that the assignment be made in writing, and that written notice of the transfer be given to the debtor. The rules of equity are less stringent but apply only to assignments for value. Equity treats an assignment as effective between assignor and assignee as soon as the assignor has done all he can to divest himself of his interest. But the assignee's security against the debtor depends on notice being given to the debtor before a further assignment. So if the owner of the debt assigns it to two people successively, the first will have no claim against the debtor if the second assignee gives notice first.

The transfer of many types of intangibles is governed by special statutory regimes. To illustrate: the Companies Acts require shares to be transferred by writing and the transfer to be registered in the books of the company, unless the company's articles of association provide otherwise. The Patents Act provides that patents be transferred by deed and that the transfer be registered in the Patents Office. The Policies of Assurance Act requires a prescribed form of words to be used to assign an insurance policy, and further requires written notice to be given to the insurance company.

149

Land

In previous chapters, we have outlined the rather complex way in which lawyers have conceptualised rights in land by comparison with their approach to rights in other things. It is not surprising then that the business of land transfer is also complex. This complexity arises at three levels. The first concerns the nature of title in English law and the plurality of ways in which it can be fragmented. The second is the existence of a number of devices through which incumbrances can be imposed upon a title, which, as we saw above, are sometimes indistinguishable from the rights which result from the process of fragmentation. The third is the existence of property rights correlative to these incumbrances on title, such as the benefit of easements and restrictive covenants. All of these facts of legal life must be provided for, and how this is done forms the subject-matter of the rest of this chapter.

Before we begin, though, let us repeat the fundamental point: the way lawyers conceptualise property grows out of the nature of their involvement with it. With land, they have long been managers of its transfer. And so the complexities discussed in previous chapters and recapitulated above are largely the product rather than the cause of what lawyers have tried to do in the course of their management of land transfer.

Most people who buy a flat on a long lease realise that they are acquiring less than full ownership of the premises, even though they may remain vague about the precise nature of their rights, and the extent to which their purchase bestows less than full ownership. But even the purchaser of a freehold house is in fact buying a fee simple in the house, or, more precisely, in the land on which the house stands. Strictly speaking, he is buying a title – a property right – to land, not the land itself.

The physical nature of land means that its ownership is likely to have passed through more hands over time than in the case of most moveables. Moreover, purchasers are potentially more vulnerable to adverse claims both because the stakes are often high and because you cannot hide land away, as you can many chattels. So, when a purchaser proposes to buy land (strictly, title to the land) he needs to ask the seller for proof that he has title. How can the seller 'prove' it? By showing how he himself acquired his title. How can he show this? Much of English land law has grown up around the range of problems embedded in this question and the search for ways of dealing with it.

In general terms, a seller of land traditionally established his title by producing the documents by means of which he acquired title from the previous owner. But this only pushed the question back one stage further. The purchaser would want to know whether that title, through which the seller derived his title, was itself a good title. How could that be proved? In exactly the same way. The seller had to produce the document through which the person from whom he had bought the land had himself derived title. Traditionally, there were two principal formalised ways through which such documentary support for the quality of a title could be marshalled, the will or last testament, and the conveyance. Although, as we shall see below, the 1925 legislation has made the traditional conveyance of title largely redundant in contemporary conditions, its nature and mode of functioning – and the problems it threw up – must all be understood if the fabric of this legislation is to be intelligible to its student today.

MECHANISMS OF LAND TRANSFER

The conveyance

The traditional method of transfer of title to land was by a conveyance – a formal legal deed which stated that by means of the deed the seller conveyed or granted his fee simple to the purchaser. The execution of the deed – the affixing of seals, etc. – itself transferred the title. It was not necessary for legal purposes that there should be a physical transfer of possession (though obviously there usually was). All that was required was the execution of the conveyance.

> The draft of the conveyance is prepared . . . by the purchaser's solicitors. It is then sent to the vendor's solicitors for approval on his behalf . . . Here it may be mentioned that when an instrument of assurance drawn by one conveyancer, whether counsel or solicitor, is sent to another to be settled on behalf of some party, whom the framer of the draft did not represent, the other should

of course make all such alterations as he considers necessary to safeguard the interests of his client: but he should not alter the draft further or otherwise than is necessary to effect this end. In short, his alterations should be directed to matters of substance only and not of form; and it is a grave breach of conveyancing etiquette for one practitioner to amend another's draft in any point, on which his client's interests would not really be affected if the instrument were to stand as originally drawn (Williams, 1922:652).

It was common, as this comment on 'protocol' suggests, for lengthy negotiation to precede a transfer of title. In modern sales of residential property, the most important question, once the price has been agreed, is to decide when the transfer will occur and when the purchase price is to be paid, so that they can arrange their affairs accordingly. All of these things are usually sorted out, prior to conveyance, by a contract. In the contract, the seller promises to sell and the buyer promises to buy and usually pays a deposit. This is the process which lawyers call 'exchange of contracts', whereas the stage of the conveyance, when title passes at law, is called completion. The contract is subject to all the normal rules of contract, and the common law remedy of damages is available for breach of it. But as we saw in Chapter 4, certain additional 'equitable' remedies are available to enforce this kind of contract, which are not normally available where a contract is for the sale of chattels.

In the past, however, the complexity of title made the preparation of the contract an arduous and sometimes hazardous affair, since it was often necessary to include a mass of special stipulations and covenants in the contract, in order to circumvent any possible dispute which might arise between the parties in the future, whether before or after completion.

Part performance

It is convenient to make a brief excursus at this point, to illustrate the particular attention which the courts of equity were willing to devote to land transactions. The Statute of Frauds of 1677, which could be said to have had the effect of keeping lawyers in employment, provided, among other things, that contracts for the sale of land required written evidence if they were to be enforceable in the courts. This generated a new problem for the equity courts. Would the absence of written evidence of an agreement for sale always defeat a purchaser who went into possession under an oral agreement and later sought, through the courts, to acquire the title deeds and a conveyance of title from a reluctant seller? Over time, the courts came to afford remedial assistance in such circumstances. The difficulty was, and to some extent remains, the question of defining with precision the circumstances in which the courts will intervene if asked. This assistance has come to be called 'the equitable doctrine of part performance'. Social and economic life, in its very nature, commonly escapes the reach of the law, which comes upon the scene only after the fact. The oral agreement which, after the statute, requires written evidence to be enforceable in court, may have been acted upon without any writing being produced. Two different problems were posed for the courts, and which problem is the more important has never been adequately resolved. On the one hand is the question which lies at the heart of much intervention by the equity courts: is there something in the dealings between the parties to the litigation which can be said to warrant the intervention of the court? This is what is meant when it is asked whether the petitioner has established an 'equity', or where, as between the disputants, the 'balance' of the equities lies. So the further the purchaser has proceeded on the basis of an oral arrangement, and acted, as we would say today, to his detriment, the more the equities move in his favour, in the sense that to put the clock back involves undoing what has been done on the basis of the bargain, in circumstances where it would be simpler, given what has happened, to compel the vendor to complete what he has promised to do, namely execute a conveyance of title in return for the payment of the purchase price.

On the other hand, the statute was concerned with the need for evidence of a contract to sell land. The things done since the making of the oral agreement – the 'acts of part performance' – can equally be viewed as making good the evidentiary deficiency caused by the absence of written evidence of the bargain. The canonical formula in which the doctrine of part performance came to be articulated at the end of the nineteenth century expresses precisely the tension between these two perspectives. It was held that the acts of part performance which would warrant court intervention must refer unequivocally to a contract concerning land. More recently it has been said that this requirement is too stringent, and that a 'balance of probabilities' test will suffice. That is, what has been done following the oral agreement does not need to persuade a court that the only explanation is that there was a contract concerning land; it is now sufficient to warrant intervention if it is more likely than not that what has been done is explicable because there was a prior agreement. What remains unresolved, so far as the scope of this jurisdiction today is concerned, is whether the court must be persuaded that the acts of part performance occurred as a result of an agreement in general, or of an agreement concerning land. It may seem plausible to a judge, for example, that one of three daughters who gives up her job and returns home to look after her ailing parents for a considerable period of time did so as the result of some arrangement between them; but is the likelihood of such an agreement sufficient for the court to invoke the doctrine, or must the court be persuaded that the arrangement was more likely than not to have concerned the family home where the parents lived, which they owned, and which the dutiful daughter claimed?

Inheritance and title

Conveyance on sale was, of course, only one of several ways in which title to land could change hands. The seller's title might have been acquired not by purchase but through inheritance. For example, his father might have bought the title, and died without selling it, but having left a will, which gave the land to his son. On his father's death, the title would vest in the executors of the will, whose job was to collect together all the property of the deceased, to pay off his debts and taxes, and then to distribute the property that was left in accordance with the directions contained in the will.

Alternatively, the father might have died leaving no will. Lawyers call this situation 'intestacy'. Here, relatives may apply to the court for letters of administration, so that they can wind up the affairs of the deceased, and then distribute the property to the next-of-kin. (The relatives who count as next-of-kin and the order of priority between them are set out in the Administration of Estates Act 1925.) If the son who is the seller in our example had acquired the title either through the will or through intestacy, a formal document known as an 'assent', which vests this title in him, would be included in the title deeds. This document proved that he had acquired title not by purchase but by succession from a purchaser.

Finally, as we have already seen, a seller's title may derive from a settlement or from the combined effect of several settlements. Such titles frequently proved to be particularly difficult to investigate.

This collection of documents of transfer, showing a chain of title being transferred from one person to another, made up what lawyers call the 'title deeds' to the property. A purchaser, in order to ensure that he got a good title, needed to check through all of these to be certain of an unbroken chain of transfers. In order to do this, he first obtained from the vendor's solicitor an 'abstract' of the vendor's title.

Abstracts of title

Evidence of title on sales being for the most part documentary, and such as can be weighed only by skilled legal advisers, it became usual to facilitate the task of judging of the effect of the title-deeds by making an abstract of their contents for the perusal of the purchaser's counsel. It appears that formerly the deeds were handed over to the purchaser for examination, and any abstract of them which he might require was made at his expense. But afterwards it became established that the vendor was bound to make at his own expense and to deliver to the purchaser an abstract of the title to the property sold . . . (Williams, 1922:97).

The abstract was to begin with identifying a good root of title, that is, with 'an instrument of disposition dealing with or proving on the face of it (without the aid of extrinsic evidence) the ownership of the whole legal and equitable estate in the property sold, containing a description by which the property can be identified, and showing nothing to cast any doubt on the title of the disposing parties' (Williams, 1922:98).

The basic idea, under this system, was that, in Sugden's words, 'wherever he begins the root of title [the solicitor] ought to abstract *every* subsequent deed' (quoted Williams, 1922:102). However, certain differences arose at this point, depending on whether it was legal or equitable rights which affected the state of the title.

With regard to documents affecting the equitable but not the legal estate in the property sold, if they be documents on which the purchaser's title will necessarily depend, they certainly ought to be placed on the abstract. But as a purchaser for value, who takes a conveyance of the legal estate in any property, is not bound by any equitable interests therein, of which he has no notice, it is obvious that there may be many documents creating equitable interests only which are not necessary to the purchaser's title, so long as he obtains the legal estate without notice of them. For instance, the vendor may be possessed of documents showing that some former owner who appeared on the face of a conveyance to be entitled for his own benefit, was in fact a trustee, or that persons who had advanced money on mortgage were trustees of the mortgage money. In such cases it would be unusual to allow notice of the trust to appear on the abstract (Williams, 1922:101).

And, as this illustrates, what came first was practical convenience. 'This . . . is no doubt a departure from the general principle', commented Williams, 'that it is for the purchaser's solicitor, and not the vendor's, to judge of the materiality of the muniments of title; but it is sanctioned by convenience and universal practice' (ibid.).

CONSEQUENCES OF THE TITLE-DEED SYSTEM

The process we have so far described was cumbersome and time-consuming. The fulcrum of the system was the conveyancing bar, the elite of the profession in the nineteenth century. It was their opinion that solicitors 'in the field' would seek if difficulties presented themselves in the course of a transaction. And it was to their opinion that judges were encouraged to defer in litigation concerning matters of establishing and transferring title. Such a system inevitably had critics. A writer in the *Edinburgh Review* of 1821 observed a paradox here:

There exists . . . an universal disinclination to the discussion of any subject purely legal; and whilst . . . all are willing to inquire and decide whether forgery shall or shall not be punished with death, few will attend to the merits of a question on a general

156

registry of title-deeds, or the alteration in the modes of transferring property: and yet, there is scarcely any person who has not experienced, in his own case, or in that of some of his connexions, considerable inconvenience from the present state of the law on these subjects. In fact, the uncertainty, the intricacy, and the variety of technical expressions, the formalities to be pursued, and the long chain of evidence to be procured, render the disposal of real property a matter of so much difficulty, that many are deterred from bringing it to market (1821:190-1).

In short, the system was so cumbersome that transfer of title was often unnecessarily difficult, or even impossible.

It is perfectly clear that transfer management took a long time and cost a lot of money. Its complexity also meant that there was a relatively high risk that transactions would fall through in the course of negotiation, or, at any rate, that people thought there was such a risk, which is just as important. But it is probably an exaggeration to suggest that the system rendered land inalienable; more accurately, the system threw up a range of problems of a purely technical character which need not have arisen if a different system had been adopted. The ingenuity of conveyancing counsel largely overcame these problems; but it was not obviously desirable or necessary to deploy the ingenuity of counsel in this way. The 1925 code stands at the end of a century of 'reform' through legislative intervention in the conveyancing process. But most of this legislation is best characterised as a vehicle for making available to all solicitors, directly, by force of statutory law, the best practice counselled by conveyancing experts in hard cases.

Beyond all the particular difficulties generated by the fragmentation of titles through the practices of settlement, and the encumbering of titles through mortgaging and leasing, was the more elementary problem generated by the fact of establishing title through a sequence of paper and parchment. On a transfer of title, the general rule was that all documents relating to the land should pass to the purchaser.

The vendor is bound, in the absence of special stipulation, to deliver over to the purchaser on completion all documents of title, which are or should rightly be in his own possession and relate solely to the property purchased, whatever be their date and whether abstracted or not. The documents, which must be so handed over, include not only the title deeds and such other muniments of title as will pass without express mention by a conveyance of the land itself, but also all documents produced for the purpose of verifying the abstract in proof of any fact stated therein; such as certificates of baptism, marriage or burial, statutory declarations as to matters of pedigree or as to the identity of the property sold, or certificates of the result of an official search for judgements or other matters. But of course documents, such as a marriage settlement, merely produced to show that they do not affect the land sold, cannot be required to be given up to the purchaser . . . (Williams, 1922:639f).

So first, what about trust documents?

Suppose that land and personality were vested in trustees by one deed of settlement, the land being settled on trust for sale, would the trustees be obliged on a sale of the land to hand over the deed of settlement to the purchaser? It is thought not . . . [However] the fact that the trustees have duties to perform under the deed, is [not] of itself sufficient to justify their retaining it. For where land alone is settled on trust for sale and the trusts of the purchase-money are declared by the same deed, it is considered that the trustees are not entitled to retain the deed of settlement on a sale of all the land; and for this reason it is the practice to declare the trusts of the purchase-money by a deed separate from the conveyance on trust for sale (ibid.: 639–41).

More seriously, what about physical fragmentation of land itself, that is, by the attempt to divide up one fee simple into several, whether by auctioning off a whole estate in lots, or simply by a landowner selling off an outlying portion of his estate? In each case, the problem was the same: the purchaser's title would derive from the vendor's title, but what arrangements needed to be made concerning the vendor's documents of title through which, subsequently, the purchaser would have to prove his own?

First, the Vendor and Purchaser Act 1874 provided that, in the absence of stipulation to the contrary, a vendor who retained any part of an estate to which any documents of title related was entitled to retain such documents. Secondly, what if documents of common title retained by the vendor contained information relating to ancillary rights burdening or benefitting the purchaser's land? We now give some examples of how lawyers in the past coped with such problems.

By the Conveyancing Act 1911, where land having a common title with other land is disposed of to a purchaser (other than a lessee or a mortgagee) who does not hold or obtain possession of the documents forming the common title, such purchaser, notwithstanding any stipulation to the contrary, may require that a memorandum giving notice of any provision contained in the disposition to him restrictive of user of, or giving rights over, any other land comprised in the common title, shall, where practicable, be endorsed on, or where impracticable, be permanently annexed to some one document selected by the purchaser but retained in the possession or power of the person who makes the disposition, and being or forming part of the common title. But the title of any person omitting to require an indorsement to be made or a memorandum to be annexed is not, by reason only of this enactment, to be prejudiced or affected by the omission (Williams, 1922:603).

Where lands held under one title are put up for sale in lots, without any special stipulation as to the custody of the title deeds, it is considered that, if all the lots be sold, the title deeds should be delivered to the purchaser of the largest part in value of the lands (whether that part be contained in one or several lots), and that he should give statutory acknowledgements and undertakings to the other purchasers . . . [More generally] the vendor is, as a rule, bound to furnish the purchaser with proper statutory acknowledgements and undertakings for the production and safe custody of any title deeds or other muniments of title which may lawfully be withheld from the purchaser on completion, and are necessary to make a good title according to the contract (ibid.:642–3).

. . . where the ownership of any land held under one title is divided, whether by sale, settlement or otherwise, and the title deeds remain in the possession of the owners of a part, the owners of the rest of the land have an equitable right, independently of any covenant, to enforce production of the title deeds in order to defend their title or effect any sale or like disposition of their lands . . . if, while the lawful custody of the deeds is outstanding (as is the case of their being in the possession of a mortgagee or a tenant for life), the title to the land devolves upon joint tenants, tenants in common, or co-parceners, or upon persons entitled in severalty to different parts of the lands, then, on the termination of the right to custody of the deeds (as by the mortgage being paid off, or the death of the tenant for life), none of them has a better right than the others to the custody of the deeds; and if they cannot agree who shall have the custody of them, the deeds will have to be deposited in Court, and each of them will be entitled to inspect and take copies of them (ibid.:645–6).

As we see in the next chapter, registration of title deeds was put forward as the solution to many of the difficulties associated with establishing title through chains of private paper kept in private hands. As we will also see, practical devices such as the separation of trust instruments from conveyances of title, which were originally invented to accommodate the difficulties we have outlined above, could then serve as a model or 'inspiration' for achieving rather different objectives.

PROOF AND INVESTIGATION OF TITLE

One of the most important historical peculiarities of the development of English land law lies in the complex relationship between, and the relative importance of, the common law courts on the one hand and the courts of equity on the other. This peculiarity is once again grounded in practical considerations, and therefore, since it is a matter of the involvement of courts in the process of transfer management by lawyers, it is a question of the remedial assistance afforded by the courts. Most of these matters, in practical terms, are today largely forgotten, but to grasp the framework of land law it is essential to understand the remedial structure of the past, because the shapes of the present are grounded upon the experience of lawyers in working within that structure.

At the heart of the tradition is the remedy of specific performance of contracts for the sale of land. For this reason, equity played a decisive role in the development of the ground-rules which contoured the activities of lawyers. These rules were reworked in 1925, as we see in the next chapter, in a comprehensive way: but the agenda of 'reform' was set by the practices of the past, and, as is inevitable in such circumstances, 'reworking' works with as well as against the way things used to be. Rather than viewing '1925' as a sudden break with the past, it must be seen as carrying forward as well as transforming the traditional practices of lawyers. In the next chapter, it is suggested that the code operated like a caesura, severing the ties that bound the present to the past. We postpone until the conclusion discussion of how these two propositions can be reconciled, or at least how each can be taken to express a part of the truth of the matter.

Specific performance was, and is, a remedy available to both parties to a contract for the sale of land. Its use threw up several issues. The first was the question of what conditions a court should impose upon a vendor before ordering specific performance of a contract of sale in his favour. This is to be distinguished from the question of what kinds of enquiries before conveyance a court of equity would require a purchaser to make. This in turn needs to be linked to the role of the court: the formulation of standards of enquiry by the courts was geared again to the availability of specific performance of the contract of sale; that is, one main type of litigation which forced the courts to formulate rules concerning the investigation of title arose out of attempts by vendors to compel purchasers to perform their contracts despite the post-contract discovery of what purchasers considered to be obstacles to title. (Of course, in the same area of doctrine, there were post-completion disputes between people asserting encumbrances on title and purchasers of the title; these too, as we shall see, tended to fall within the province of equity.) To get such contract litigation into perspective, we should note that it is not fundamentally a matter of people refusing to perform contracts *tout court*; rather, it is often the more 'technical' question of (a) purchasers whose advisers are unwilling to proceed to completion because they do not think the vendor has shown or can give title, once the abstract has been investigated; (b) purchasers who are unwilling to proceed because some defect – like an underground water course – has been discovered in the land itself which in the purchaser's view materially alters the bargain to the extent that he wishes to rescind the contract.

'Good title': what vendors had to show

. . . every vendor of land is bound to show a good title to the property sold by him. This rule would appear to be of equitable origin. The courts of equity, in granting to a vendor the extraordinary relief of enforcing specific performance of the contract, considered that it was only fair to impose the condition, that he on his side should prove that he could actually convey what he professed to sell. [The law came to follow equity here.] What the vendor has to prove, in order to fulfil this obligation, is that he can convey that which he contracted to sell . . . But the nature and extent of proof required was defined by a general rule of equity and law, adopted from the practice of conveyancers, whereby proof of title for not less than sixty years before the contract was held to be proof of a good title, if nothing appeared to the contrary. . . . (Williams, 1922:88–9).

Williams called this merely a 'subordinate rule' which limited the amount of evidence a purchaser could require.

It simply bound the purchaser to accept, as proof of a good title, evidence of sixty years' ownership ending in the vendor . . . provided, however, that nothing appeared to show that the ownership so proved was not full or complete. But it was of no avail to show sixty years' title, if the result of the evidence produced were not to discharge the vendor's main obligation, that is, that he could actually convey what he sold (ibid.:88–9).

Williams insisted upon 'this apparently simple distinction between the main rule imposing the duty of showing a good title, that is, a title to convey what was sold, and the subordinate rule defining the manner of proof' (1922:89)

. . . omission to remember this distinction has been a fruitful source of error, especially in cases where *the time* for which title can be required to be shown has been limited by special stipulation [in the contract for sale]. In some such cases, the vendors, or their advisers, would appear to have forgotten that such a stipulation merely limits the evidence of title that can be asked of them in the first instance, and does not exempt them from the general duty of proving that they have the right to convey what they have sold (ibid.:89–90).

If the contract contains a special stipulation for a shorter period of proof than that specified by the general law, the stipulation '. . . must be fair and explicit, or the vendor, in seeking specific performance, will not be allowed to insist on it.' (ibid.:100).

> If . . . a stipulation be made that the title shall commence with a particular deed less than forty years old, the purchaser is entitled to assume that the deed was made on an occasion on which the title would be investigated; and should this not be the case, as if the deed were voluntary, the vendor cannot force him, in an action for specific performance, to accept the title as limited by the condition. Such conditions, to be effectual as regards the specific performance of the contract, must clearly state the nature of the instrument, with which the title is to commence (ibid.:100–1).

In 1874, a forty-year period was substituted by statute, which was reduced to thirty years in 1925, and in 1969 was further shortened to fifteen years. Let us examine this more closely through an example.

EXAMPLE
(1) Thirty years ago, A conveys to B;
(2) Twenty years ago, B conveys to C;
(3) Thirteen years ago, C conveys to D;
(4) Today, D is planning to sell to P.
How far back must P check the title? He must look at the series of conveyances going back for at least fifteen years. So he must look at (3). But he must also look at (2) because he must go back to that conveyance, through which D derives his title, made at least fifteen years ago.

If he does not look at (2) this does not mean that the transfer from D is bad. It means that his title is at risk because he has not looked at the title deeds going back to transfer (2). Therefore, he is liable to attack from people in whose favour adverse interests were created by B. The other side of the rule – that he takes a good title if he does go back to (2) – means that the purchaser is not concerned with interests adverse to the title which could only be discovered by going back to (1). The rule, therefore, does not require him to go back to (2), nor to (1), but the consequence of failing to check (1) or (2) are different. Because of the rule, failure to check (2) may expose him to

163

attack from third parties, but failure to go back to (1) will not. However, as we see in the next chapter, the introduction of registration of land charges in 1925 has complicated the position.

Good title and the limitation of actions

Williams again:

> . . . the Court will compel a purchaser to take a title depending . . . on the extinguishment under [the Limitation Acts] of the right and title of some person . . . who [is] shown to have been rightfully entitled. But it must not be supposed that this doctrine enables a vendor, who has been in possession for twelve or even thirty years to escape the common obligation of showing forty years' title as proof of a good title. Possession for these periods does not give a good title under the [Limitation Acts] as against all the world; it does not bar the rights of remaindermen or reversioners not entitled to possession until the determination of some particular estate. It does not appear therefore that a vendor's obligation of showing a good title can be discharged by proof of thirty or even forty years' possession by himself alone, without showing, if the Statute of Limitations be relied on, who were rightfully entitled and that the vendor's possession has effectually barred their claims (Williams, 1922:96–7).

WHAT PURCHASERS HAD TO DO: INVESTIGATING TITLE AND CONSTRUCTIVE NOTICE

It must always be remembered that the courts of equity were principally geared to the resolution of disputes, rather than, as we too easily suppose today (precisely because of the routinisation of practice facilitated by improved communication networks within the legal system) the making of legal rules. Just as the rules concerning what vendors should do were parasitic upon – or grew out of litigation about – attempts by vendors to get specific performance of contracts for the sale of land, so the rules which emerged concerning purchasers were generated by disputes concerning either purchasers' attempts to tear up ('rescind') such contracts (where there was dispute at a more basic level as to whether this was a matter for law or for equity (Williams, 1922:154n.(d)) or by disputes between those who claimed as encumbrancers upon the vendor's title and the purchaser. The reach of equitable remedial assistance tended to stop, though not in every case, where the defendant could satisfy the court that he was a 'bona fide purchaser of a legal estate without notice' of the claim asserted in the court. 'Notice', in other words, was formulated in the context of land purchase, and came to involve positing a standard of enquiry into the state of a (legal) title to land. For this reason, the opinion of conveyancing experts was so important for the development of this equitable 'doctrine'.

Let us assume that A has the legal estate in Blackacre, and B has some equitable interest affecting the land (either an estate contract with A, or a restrictive covenant). A conveys the legal estate to P. The contest in the courtroom is between B and P, A for whatever reasons having dropped out of the picture.

What did it mean to say that A 'knew or ought to have known' of B's equitable interest? Obviously, the 'equitable interest' is not a physical, tangible, observable thing. Rather it is a right which arose originally because equity was prepared to grant B certain kinds of remedies against A because A's conscience was bound by what had happened between A and B.

First, B might argue that P actually knew of the prior relationship between A and B – that they had made a restrictive covenant or an estate contract. If B can produce evidence to the court to this effect, P's conscience will be bound in the same way as A's conscience was – in modern language, P will therefore take subject to B's rights. This is called actual notice.

Secondly, the evidence may not extend so far as to prove actual knowledge on the part of P, but B may be able to argue that P would have found out about his equitable interest if he had made the proper enquiries before taking the conveyance from A.

B is thus positing a standard of reasonable enquiry, and it is for the court to decide what this standard should be. This is called constructive notice – B is not arguing that P actually knew (actual notice) but that P ought to have known about his equitable interest because if P had come up to the standard of the reasonable purchaser, P would, in the course of his pre-conveyance investigations, have 'discovered' B's equitable interest.

So what is this standard of reasonable enquiry which equity imposed upon a purchaser before he could take free of equitable interests which might affect the land?

Essentially, purchasers were required to make two different kinds of enquiry – first, to inspect the land, and secondly, to investigate the title deeds.

Investigative procedures

INSPECTION OF THE LAND

As a general rule if a person purchases and takes a conveyance of an estate which he knows to be in the occupation of another than the vendor, he is bound by all the equities which the person in such occupation may have in the land; for possession is prima facie seisin, and the purchaser has, therefore, actual notice of a fact by which the property is affected, and he is bound to ascertain the truth. Thus, if a person purchases property in the occupation of one whom he supposes to be only a tenant from year to year, he will be held to have notice of a lease under which he holds, and of the contents of it (Hewitt and Richardson, 1928:195).

When a purchaser inspects the land which he is proposing to buy, he may discover that people other than the legal owner are in occupation or doing certain things on that land. This will 'put him on enquiry', which means that he should find out what, if any, their rights in relation to the land are. If he does not enquire, and it subsequently turns out that these people have equitable interests affecting the land, the purchaser will take subject to those equitable interests.

EXAMPLE A, the owner of land in fee simple, makes an agreement with some builders (B) such that the builders acquire by virtue of the agreement an equitable interest in the land. As a result of this agreement, P, the purchaser, would have discovered, had he inspected the land, that much building activity was taking place upon it. This puts P on enquiry about the nature of B's rights, and P is therefore fixed with constructive notice of the builders' equitable interest, and made to take subject to the agreement.

166

INVESTIGATION OF THE TITLE DEEDS

We have already seen that the law has at different times laid down minimum periods for searching through the title deeds in order for the purchaser to get good title. As he looks through these conveyances, he may come across other documents which indicate that there are also equitable interests affecting the land. If we return to the example on page 163, C, who acquired the land twenty years ago, may have entered into a restrictive covenant in favour of his neighbour X. This is an equitable interest, as we have seen, and X will be able to enforce it against P if P has actual notice of the covenant because he came across it when looking through the title deeds. But if P has not discovered it, or has shut his eyes to its existence, then he will be taken to have constructive notice of the covenant if he should have discovered it had he searched the title deeds properly (i.e. as a reasonable purchaser).

The same principles applied in the case of other equitable interests which we have already discussed. Thus, in searching through the title deeds, P might discover that a trust had been created at some point, and this should lead him to enquire whether the beneficial interests behind that trust still affected the title. Similarly, he might discover that V had made a previous estate contract if he came across some memorandum in the title deeds to put him on enquiry.

It was questions of this sort – technical questions, conveyancers' questions – which established the 'agenda of reform' to which, shortly, we turn. We must first outline the relationship between the recognition of a range of ancillary rights and the process of transfer management.

LEASES AND THE TRANSFER OF TITLE

We have indicated above how a lease of land could itself be the object of a transfer of title. Leases became things which people bought and sold, as well as things to be 'checked out' when a superior title was transferred. We have already outlined that aspect of leases which was, and is, relatively peculiar, namely that leases tend to contain ongoing covenants relating to the use of the property. In legal terms, the transfer of leases – the 'assignment of leases' as lawyers call it – is largely a matter of ensuring that the covenants contained in the lease bind (and benefit) the person who takes an assignment of the lease. As between landlord and tenant, covenants remain enforceable if they 'touch and concern the land' or if they have reference to the subject matter of the lease. Here the position of tenants derives from common law and that of landlords from statute, in each case from long ago.

LAND TRANSFER AND THE CREATION OR TRANSFER OF RIGHTS ANCILLARY TO TITLE

The discussion to this point has centred upon the interplay of fragmentation of title and the management of land transfer by lawyers. We have focused so far upon the problems of ascertaining the quality of title and the nature of the incumbrances upon that title. But one can look at this process the other way round: what exactly did a purchaser get when he bought an estate in land? How much of what belonged to the vendor passed with the conveyance? At one level, this problem was elementary and easily dealt with at the contract stage: what fixtures would pass with the transfer of title?

The general rule was that anything which was fixed or attached to the land was treated as being part of the land, and so passed on a conveyance of title unless the contract contained express stipulations to contrary effect. Conversely, anything not attached could be removed by the vendor on completion since it was still a chattel. It was for conveyancers to ascertain, during the transfer negotiations, what the contracting parties' intentions were regarding items like machinery bolted to the ground for the purposes of use but in fact regarded by the seller as moveables which he would take away with him. Ornaments were also the source of complexity in adjudication. The courts took the view that on the one hand large pictures fixed to a wall 'for their better enjoyment' retained their chattel character, while pictures or sculptures which came to form part of an overall architectural design became part of the land whether or not they were actually attached to it. However peripheral such matters may seem today, they were once real issues on the transfer and break-up of landed estates, as the law reports reveal.

It is the recognition by English law of proprietary rights ancillary to title, examined in the previous chapter, which added complexity here. Leaving aside prescriptive rights, the creation of land obligations was commonly linked to the transfer of title and to the subdivision of large parcels of land in particular. Where land was divided up for residential development, or where an outlying portion of an agricultural estate was sold off to raise money, the question of whether obligations should be attached to one or other of the parcels of land arose. In the case of covenants, the question had to be addressed explicitly; in the case of easements, as we see in a moment, it could also arise as a matter of (retrospective) imposition.

The principal mechanism for making rights and obligations run with the land is called by lawyers 'annexation'. The word expresses the 'materialist' or 'reifying' way in which conveyancers have tended to think about rights and obligations. Where the benefit and burden of an easement or a restrictive covenant, or the benefit of a positive covenant, is annexed to the land, it thereafter 'runs' with the land. This was of course literally true under the title-deed system, provided that a copy of the easement or covenant was made. Such easement or covenant is treated as a thing because one can literally ask where it is; and if it cannot be produced it cannot be enforced. So if the owner of a large parcel conveyed an outlying part to a purchaser, taking a restrictive covenant from him to use the land for residential purposes only, or granting or reserving him an easement over the vendor's retained land, the easement or covenant would live on in the title deeds of the purchaser. The vendor, in such circumstances, would need to keep a copy, if only to prevent fraud in the future, and this copy would form part of the vendor's subsequent title deeds. Clearly, in such a system, future division of either parcel of land could necessitate complex arrangements regarding rights to production of the relevant pieces of paper and parchment.

How does annexation occur? Again the answer is in the use of the correct formula, one devised by lawyers to indicate both that the benefit of the covenant was not personal to the covenantee and was taken in order to benefit the land. If the benefit of a restrictive covenant was not annexed, equity permitted the covenantee to pass on the benefit on a sale of the land by assignment, that is, the conveyance on sale would expressly refer to the covenant and contain express words of assignment: another formula again. . . .

Easements could also arise by implication. After a conveyance of title on the sale of an outlying part, the question could arise whether the grant or reservation of any easements should be implied into a conveyance even if there was nothing said expressly. Here the courts did come to formulate a number of principles.

The basis for implying easements into transfers of title has recently been said to be the intention of the parties to the transfer. This has been broken down into three alternative formulations: the common intention of the parties, necessity, and what is known as the rule in *Wheeldon v. Burrows* (1879).[20] The first two justifications for implying easements into a transfer of title require little comment. The circumstances will usually speak for themselves. Because, however, the basis underpinning the implication of easements is the intention of the parties to the transaction and not some 'public policy' promoting the better utilization of land, the implication of an easement can always be prevented by an express stipulation excluding it, even if the effect of such an exclusion is to render the land in question completely inaccessible to human beings because it is completely surrounded by land owned by other people.

The third basis for implying easements, formulated in *Wheeldon v. Burrows*, implies into a conveyance as easements any 'rights' which were continuous and apparent at the time of the conveyance which are necessary for the reasonable enjoyment of the land.

Finally, section 62 of the Law of Property Act 1925 is sometimes treated in the books as a fourth method of implying easements into transfers of title. This section writes into every transfer what are sometimes called the 'general words'. The section does not imply easements into a transfer so much as save words by writing them in by force of statute (a point to which we return in the next chapter). As with most such statutory provisions, it is subject to a contrary intention being expressed in the conveyance, which means that it both saves words and focuses the minds of the parties on whether they wish to exclude anything from passing along with the transfer of title.

8

The Mechanics of Land Transfer: the 1925 Reforms

The process of land transfer in England is now regulated by what is commonly regarded as the finest flower of codification *à l'anglaise*, the 1925 code of property legislation. This code operated as a caesura; it caused a certain rupture with the past. Several reasons for this can be suggested. First, the code is extremely long and complicated, and in its early years required a considerable effort to master. There was pressure to give particular sections some fixed meaning. In a general climate of slavish adherence to precedent (1930s–1950s), there were strong incentives to follow previous interpretations, regardless of whether they were right or wrong (that is, irrespective of whether or not they conformed to the received wisdom of the nineteenth century). Secondly, the legislation was in some respects the victim of its own success; inasmuch as it ironed out technical problems which had vexed nineteenth-century lawyers, the past came to seem a terrain best left undisturbed, the province of antique collectors, not practical men. Thirdly, coming to more modern times, practising lawyers by the 1950s had little direct experience of the pre-1926 years, and were encouraged in their happy ignorance by the most influential textbook writers (Anderson, 1984). Finally, the world of real property seemed to have changed. How could the learning of the nineteenth century provide guidance on the scope of the Rent Acts, or in disputes among the 'families' of owner-occupiers?

What sort of animal was the 1925 code? It resembled, in the kind of thing it was, what went before. It was a bundle of particulars. This code contained no definitions of dominium, usufructs, servitudes or hypothecs, of the kind familiar to civilians. It was a body of particular rules of a particular kind. They were conveyancing rules. Rules for regulating the transfer of title to land, as well as mostly procedural rules governing legal relationships where land

171

was, to put the matter generally, in 'multiple ownership'. Not that these rules were, or are, unimportant. Generations of lawyers have treated them with the utmost respect, even reverence, because the meat of our law of real property (at least, that part of it which matters to lawyers in their day-to-day activities) is in these rules. The rules are a sort of highway code, the rules of the road telling lawyers how to go about their business, the do's and don't's of making wills, leases, trusts, of buying and selling houses. Some of the most important rules (in a practical sense) amount to this: if you transfer title to a house to someone, you will be taken to have transferred to that person along with the house this, that and the other (say, the hedges, ditches and fences that are reputed to be part of that piece of land) unless you have expressly stated in your transfer that they are not being transferred. Such provisions are called 'word-saving' clauses because that is what they do. They simplify the preparation of the relevant legal instruments. They cut down on the paperwork. And dealing with paperwork – interpreting the meaning of words used in legal documents – is in large measure how the English law of real property has grown up. If you use this word but omit that word, you are taken to have done this but not that. So next time round, a lawyer whose client wants to do both this and that must ensure that he uses this word and that word. The effectiveness of such a system always depended ultimately upon the adequacy of information flows between the people who prepared the documents and the people who interpreted them in the event of a dispute about meaning. Of course, given that lawyers everywhere have a reputation for splitting hairs, such a system tended towards overkill. A kind of verbal inflation resulted. Legal instruments became longer and longer. More and more words, representing every conceivable shade of meaning, were included, in case the omission of any one should prove fatal later on. One important function of conveyancing statutes like the 1925 code was to bring these verbal formulae into the statutory text, impose them upon all private instruments by force of law, unless those preparing the instrument wished to exclude something (which in most cases they would not). Beyond that, the 1925 code was an elaborate reworking of the old law on settlements and trusts of land. It addressed, almost completely successfully, nineteenth-century problems in order to make the transfer of title to land subjected to complex settlements more straightforward. This has had to serve as the legal framework in the very different world of widespread owner-occupation. English property law, then, as 'codified' in 1925, did not consist of a definitive statement of property rights and their incidents, but rather a set of rules focused on the procedures and mechanisms of land transfer. This deposited a new, generalized ideological centrepiece into legal culture 'created', it would seem, by academic lawyers but adopted, in more recent years, by practitioners and judges. This is 'the policy of 1925' which is said, in general but humdrum terms, to consist of the 'simplification and facilitation of conveyancing', or, in more glamorous but old-fashioned language, 'free trade in land'. That this became an ideological centrepiece of legal culture must be stressed, because it is only marginally connected with more general political ideologies relating to the merits or demerits of private property rights. In brief, 'the policy of 1925' in legal discourse was targeted at adjudication: it functioned as a mode of legitimating those interpretations or applications of the 1925 code which 'simplified' or 'facilitated' conveyancing – i.e. land transfer – and of delegitimating those which pulled in the direction of greater complexity. In other words, as an ideological theme it was very much concerned with the office work of lawyers (and of solicitors in particular) with the paperwork they would or would not have to do in the preparation of land transfer documentation.

For our purposes, the main statutes are: the Settled Land Act 1925 (SLA); the Law of Property Act 1925 (LPA); the Land Charges Act 1925 (now Land Charges Act 1972, LCA); and the Land Registration Act 1925 (LRA). The first three of these Acts changed a few substantive rules and modified some aspects of the traditional conveyancing practices of transfer by title deed, the general character of which was outlined in the previous chapter. The LRA introduced a new system of conveyancing, which we now call registered conveyancing. This was intended to speed up and simplify the process of land transfer by making it easier for purchasers to investigate the title they were buying, and to find out whether there were subsidiary rights burdening the land they were buying (like restrictive covenants and easements). The traditional conveyancing procedures (which today we call unregistered conveyancing) were thought to be too cumbersome, despite the streamlining introduced by the LPA and the LCA, and the advocates of registered conveyancing hoped that it would supersede the old title deed system. At the time of writing, it seems probable that there will be unregistered titles left after the year 2000.

As was noted in previous chapters, this legislation made considerable inroads into the conceptual framework of property law, especially so far as the distinction between legal and equitable rights is concerned. But since the underlying rationale of these modifications is explicable only in terms of the management by lawyers of land transfer, detailed exploration of these changes has been postponed until this point. The key targets of the 1925 legislation were, for present purposes, twofold: to overcome the fragmentation of title to land (see Chapter 3 above) and to reform the mechanics of land transfer (see Chapter 7 above). Before these are outlined, we must enter an important qualification concerning the character of what follows.

Apart from the pioneering work of Avner Offer (1977), very little research has been published on the 'real history' of the 1925 legislation. As a result, we know very little about why particular provisions were adopted rather than others. So it is difficult to know to what wider issues the history of this legislation should be linked. (For some suggestions, see Murphy and Clark, 1983:16–17 and notes.) Because we know so little about these matters, it is difficult to say what date is best taken as the starting point of this history. Offer started his detailed study in 1910, and located the starting point of the movement for conveyancing reform in the late nineteenth century. But viewed more generally, the project of reforming English conveyancing has a much longer pedigree. Even if the author writing in the *Edinburgh Review* quoted in the previous chapter proclaimed himself to be a lonely voice in 1821, by the end of that decade, Parliament had set Commissioners to work on the reform of the law of Real Property and voluminous reports were produced in due course. The statute book of the nineteenth century is littered with Acts concerned with this or that aspect of conveyancing practice. In the form in which it finally emerged, large parts of the 1925 legislation were more – much more – of the same. As already indicated, the 1925 code sought to be comprehensive, but ended up being as comprehensive as it could be by being particularistic. It contains its generalities to be sure – including those selected for discussion here, the new regime for strict settlements and tenancies in common – but even so, the SLA ran to 117 pages, which made it longer than the LRA, which weighed in at 106. (The LPA was a bloated 203 pages.) Among other things, of course, this is suggestive of what the priorities were of those who successfully piloted through the version of the code with which we now have to live (see Offer, 1977).

The origin of the project of reforming – or abolishing – strict settlements is equally difficult to pinpoint, but it can be traced back well into the nineteenth century, at very least to 1880 (cf. Brodrick, 1881). In other words, the principal limbs of the 1925 'scheme' singled out here for discussion seem to have their roots firmly in the nineteenth century. It may well be that, when we know more about its genesis, we shall come to see it as one of the last flowerings of the Victorian age, as capacious as its buildings, as draughty, and as difficult to adapt for modern living.

So the reader will not find answered here the question why these targets, introduced above and outlined below, were selected, because we are not in a position to give it. The 'explanation' offered here resembles more closely one of the justifications offered at the time by conveyancers, namely that the reforms addressed the problem of the fragmentation of title to land. But this must not be confused with the suggestion that there was some Grand Plan which we can wrap up and label 'the Policy of 1925'. Whether there was or was not, as we have said, we do not know. At best, in the state of present knowledge, we suggest that this is improbable. Given the number of people involved, which we know in part from Offer, and the time over which the various bills laid before Parliament stretch (wherever one begins the story), it is much more likely that the final product was an amalgam of several plans, some grander than others, a conclusion at which any reader of the legislation will quickly arrive. There is nothing odd about this; it is a general, much observed, and very longstanding feature of the British mode of legislating.

Inevitably, since we do not have this real history, it is difficult to tell in what way if at all it would assist the student of the legislation were it to be produced. Knowing which conveyancer was responsible for which section is 'interesting', but it may not much help the student who is struggling to work out what it means, or why, in a larger sense, it is there. As indicated above, what follows is a commentary on certain critical aspects of the text of 1925, and the explanation we present is best read as the kind of answer we can imagine the person responsible for the item under discussion would have given if asked the question, 'What is the point of this?' That is why, throughout this book, we have tried to give some impression or 'feel' of the world, now passed, of those who wrote these statutes. Inevitably, the contours of this world are drawn in the recesses of these statutes, and these reflect the experience of the past, because most of the time, when people seek to make the future, they have available to them only the materials they have inherited. As we shall see, even the 'new age' regime of registered conveyancing suggests that the final product does not escape the truth of this generalisation.

1925: SETTLEMENT AND THE QUALITY OF TITLE

The reform of the strict settlement: the Settled Land Acts 1882–1925

The Settled Land Acts revolved around giving the tenant for life an unfettered power of sale over the land. The 1882 Act did simply this; the 1925 scheme goes further by stipulating that the legal fee simple absolute in possession must be vested in the tenant for life. To follow this scheme through, it is necessary in addition to cease to recognise at law any other freehold estates in land.

So, after 1925, lesser estates (life estate, entail) and all future estates (remainders, reversions) can exist only in equity behind a trust. The planning of inheritance could continue, but now without fragmenting the title. Finally, if the tenant for life is to be given effective control over the title, how are the interests of the family to be protected? By ensuring that purchase monies are not paid to the tenant for life on a sale but to separate, independent trustees – the 'Trustees of the Settlement'.

The reform of the tenancy in common

As a mode of settling land and predetermining inheritance, the tenancy in common was less ambitious regarding the future (it involved only minimal planning, whereas strict settlements involved rigid planning and prioritizing of family claims); but it was much more troublesome in its effect on the state of the title. Tenancy in

176

common was a mode of parcelling rental income from an estate, of sharing it out between a number of people concurrently entitled. Over time, each share could become subdivided. The title could always be dealt with on the market by all such tenants acting together; but over time, (i) a purchaser inspecting the title might be unsure whether he had the aggregate of the right individuals; (ii) some of these individuals might be infants; (iii) some of the shares might be encumbered by mortgages; (iv) some of the 'shareholders' might be recalcitrant and even the smallest would have, in effect, a veto over dealing with the title.

It is essential to recall that this was the rentier's settlement *par excellence.* It was simply a way of distributing rental income among a family. Its functional character provides the key to the way the reformers dealt with its defects, as they appeared to conveyancers.

1. The legal tenancy in common was abolished so that serious fragmentation of title ceased. The sharing out of money derived from land was now to be achieved through equity – i.e. equitable tenants in common operating behind a trust.

2. But how was the legal title (the fee simple absolute in possession) to be held? In this form of settlement, there was no real equivalent to the tenant for life (the head of the family) of the strict settlement. But since genealogical seniority played no part in the rationale of the tenancy in common, and since a trust could be used to protect the claims of the 'shareholders', the problem could be resolved in an arbitrary way: where a will or conveyance tried to create a legal tenancy in common, up to the first four persons named would hold the title as legal 'joint tenants' on 'trust for sale' for all the persons named as equitable tenants in common.

3. This requires us to examine (a) the joint tenancy; (b) the (statutory) trust for sale.

4. In the 1925 scheme, the joint tenancy becomes the only permitted form of concurrent ownership in respect of the legal title. Its advantage, from a conveyancing point of view, concerns what happens on the death of a joint tenant: as we noted in Chapter 3, his or her interest simply disappears or is engulfed by those of the surviving joint tenants. Since only estates held in common could be transmitted by inheritance, joint tenants sometimes tried to convert their joint tenancies into tenancies in common. This is called 'severance'. After 1925, it is impossible to sever a joint tenancy of the legal

estate; it can happen only in equity, behind the trust.

5. Given the original nature of the tenancy in common, a special statutory framework was required to regulate the relations between the 'shareholders' once their substantial entitlements were to be pushed away from the title and behind a trust. This was found in the trust for sale. A trust was imposed by statute (the 'statutory trust for sale') whose nature was modelled on a pre-existing device, the 'express' trust for sale, which was well-established by the nineteenth century.

For example, someone owning four or five houses which were rented out might, in his will, leave them to trustees on trust for sale, the proceeds of sale to be divided equally among his children, and, pending sale, the rental income to be similarly apportioned. This provided the model. In place of the legal tenancy in common, a statutory trust for sale would arise. Pending sale, the income from the property would be payable to the equitable tenants in common by virtue of those interests, and, on sale, the proceeds divided between them. If the 'shareholders' were in disagreement over the desirability of a sale, the court was given a discretion to say yes or no. (LPA 1925, section 30). The precise powers of the trustees, broadly modelled on those of the SLA tenant for life, were also established by statute (in the LPA 1925).

The two-trustee rule, 'overreaching' and notice

These reforms, targeted at the fragmentation of title, pushed all the sources of complexity behind trusts. But if purchasers were to be affected by notice of these (now) beneficial interests, the old problems could recur in a new form. In particular, a purchaser might be unwilling to proceed even though the legal title was in good order unless the beneficiaries concurred in the transfer. So it was necessary to devise procedures for circumventing such difficulties. The broad scheme to eliminate notice of trusts from conveyancing – which underpins the entire code – was that a purchaser who obtained a receipt for the proceeds of sale from two trustees would not be concerned with the beneficial interests in the land. Those interests, it is usually said, are, in such circumstances, 'overreached' into the proceeds of sale, and the land is thereby freed from the claims of the beneficiaries. Who these trustees would be would differ in the case of the two new devices for dealing with settlements of land: in the case of the SLA settlement, the trustees of the settlement; in the case of the statutory trust for sale, the trustees for sale.

The effects of these reforms can now be summarized schematically:

1. Almost all land held on trust must be held either under the Settled Land Act scheme or on a trust for sale within the LPA.[21]

2. Where land is held on trust (subject to the exceptions referred to in the above note):

(a) Who gives title?

   (i) In a SLA settlement, the tenant for life has the legal estate.
   (ii) In a trust for sale, the trustees for sale have the legal estate.

(b) Who gives a receipt for the purchase price?

   (i) In a SLA settlement, the trustees of the settlement receive the purchase price.
   (ii) In a trust for sale, the trustees for sale receive the purchase price.

3. When is land held on a trust for sale and when does the SLA apply?

(a) Where there are –

   (i)   successive beneficial interests subsisting and
   (ii) no trust for sale was expressly created in the original grant, and
   (iii) the beneficial interests in possession are not held under a tenancy in common,
   – the SLA will apply.

(b) Where a legal estate is granted to trustees expressly on trust for sale, there will be an express trust for sale.

(c) Where –

   (i) the beneficial interest in possession is concurrently held by A and B as tenants in common (whether or not there are remainders over), and
   (ii) there is no express trust for sale (see (b) above)
        – the land will be held on a statutory trust for sale.

This was designed to accommodate the practice sometimes adopted in settlements of land [discussed above on pages 66-7 and 70] of passing the family estates to the daughters of the tenant for life as (legal) tenants in common in the event of a failure in the male line. Consistency required that this practice too should cease so that such tenancies in common could only take effect, like any other, behind a trust. Since the passing of the family estates to daughters as tenants in common had always involved the probability of an eventual breaking up of those estates, the obvious form that the trust should now take, in the absence of express provision, was a statutory trust for sale (cf. Murphy and Clark, 1983:90).

(d) Where –

   (i)   the beneficial interest in possession is concurrently held by A and B as joint tenants, and

   (ii) there is no express trust for sale, and

   (iii) there are no remainders over (so that A and B are joint owners of the equitable fee simple absolute in possession)
      – the land will be held on a statutory trust for sale.

This was designed with the rather modest objective of providing practical mechanisms for future land transfer and dispute resolution (e.g. over the desirability of a sale). But, almost by accident, it has turned out to be of central importance today as the legal framework regulating co-owned and occupied residential property. This is because of the modern development of the implied trust, discussed in Chapter 4. Where such a trust arises under the 'general principles' of equity, the courts have held that it comes within this part of the 1925 scheme for dealing with settlements, so that the equitable shares will operate behind a statutory trust for sale, and the relationship between the parties will be governed by the statutory machinery.

1925:REFORMING THE MECHANICS
OF INVESTIGATION OF TITLE

As should now be clear, by the beginning of this century 'land-ownership' meant, for most of those people in a position to think about such matters, ownership or shared ownership of a bundle of documents (wills, conveyances on sale, deeds of settlement) of title. Atiyah (1978) has observed – with the 'law' of contract in mind – that common lawyers tend to 'reification' in their thinking: they talk about a contract as if it were a 'thing' rather than a bundle of rights and correlative obligations. Whether or not his criticism is helpful, his diagnosis is accurate, and it is even more true of the law of property. When lawyers spoke of 'the title', they had in mind not some mystical entity like the civil lawyer's *dominium* but the tangible, messy, and inordinately verbose collection of documents which did not just stand for, represent or prove the title but in every practical sense (and there was no other for the common lawyer) were the title.

The traditional mode of land transfer on sale which went with this mode of constituting title goes by the grand name of 'conveyance by private treaty'. As we have seen, it was in essence up to the lawyers acting for each side to satisfy themselves, on behalf of their clients, that everything was in order. The main scope of intervention by the courts (and thus the main opportunity in this area for the formulation of something approaching rules of 'law' – i.e. public, general rules applicable to everyone: judge-made law is necessarily 'public law' in that sense) came as a result of disputes arising after exchange of contracts concerning what terms needed to be included in the conveyance in order to fulfil the obligations created by the contract.

Here, as elsewhere, history is just a succession of things which could have been otherwise. Title, its constitution, proof and transfer, could have been, as it was elsewhere, a public, not a private, matter. Land transfer could have been organised by the state. And by the end of the nineteenth century, this had been set in motion, through the establishment of a Registry of Titles, for the County of London. In 1925, this system could have been made available to the country as a whole. That it was not is tribute to the political acumen of the then leaders of the Law Society. The Land Registration Act of 1925 did introduce a nationwide scheme for registration of title and thus state-organised land transfer. But its implementation was to be by administrative action, different geographical areas to be brought within the new system when the Lord Chancellor so determined. Only today are we approaching the time when the whole country is to be governed by the new system. As a transitional measure (one of the longest transitions in our legal history) a modified version of the old system was established in 1925 in the Land Charges Act 1925 (now 1972). The introduction of a 'Public' Register of Titles did not involve the creation of a register open to inspection by members of the public. Here too the values and assumptions of the old system were carried through into the new. Just as under the title-deed system, the documents of title were in private hands and access to the information contained in them basically required the permission of their owner, so in the registered system, although the information was held by public officials, they would disclose it only if the owner so permitted.

The reformed old system: alphabetical indexation of encumbrances in name of estate owner

The Land Charges Act established a procedure which involved setting up a national Register of Land Charges, and drawing up a list, contained in the LCA, of the kinds of equitable interests which are registrable. This list includes estate contracts and restrictive covenants.

Someone who has a registrable interest such as a restrictive covenant is to register the interest against the name of the estate owner who has created the covenant in his favour. The Land Charges Register is simply an alphabetical list of the names of all estate owners against whom interests have been registered. When a purchaser examines the title deeds, he will see the names of all the previous estate owners prior to the seller (through whom the seller traces title). The purchaser must then fill in a form which is sent to the Land Charges Registry asking whether any equitable interests have been entered in the register against those names. This is known as a search of the register. If the Registry writes back and informs P of various interests which have been entered, P does in reality have actual notice of those rights, and takes subject to them if he goes ahead with the conveyance.

Estate contracts were also brought within the same procedure of registration. Obviously, though, the practical effect of registration may be different as between estate contracts and restrictive covenants. If P discovers through his search a restrictive covenant affecting the property, he may still go ahead and take a conveyance. This will depend on why he is buying the property, and the use to which he wishes to put it. If, however, he discovers an estate contract, he is likely to back out of a conveyance, because, if he takes a conveyance of the legal title from the seller, he is unlikely to acquire anything of value, since the estate contract will be enforceable against him.

What if B had the benefit of a restrictive covenant (i.e. the right under the old law to enforce it against a purchaser with notice) but had not registered it, so that P's search of the register would not disclose the existence of the covenant? The rule here was that failure to register a registrable interest (like a restrictive covenant) made it void (i.e. of no legal effect) as against a purchaser of the legal estate for money or money's worth. This means that even though a purchaser has actual notice under the old law of the existence of the restrictive covenant (e.g. by investigating the title deeds) the covenant cannot be enforced against the purchaser because it has not been registered.

The basic principle to grasp is that entry of a land charge on the Register constitutes actual notice to the whole world of the existence of that equitable interest, which means that any purchaser will take subject to it.

For present purposes, two problems need to be mentioned. First, if a purchaser fills in a search form and sends it to the Registry, the official certificate which he receives in reply from the Registry is conclusive as to what equitable interests affect the land. So if the Registry is careless and overlooks a charge which has been entered against the name of one of the estate owners mentioned in P's search form, that official certificate from the Registry, because it is conclusive, takes precedence over the fact of registration.

In other words, although registration counts as actual notice to the whole world, a slip in the Registry can lead to a purchaser taking free of a registered interest, because the Registry's certificate to the purchaser cannot be challenged later. This means that if the person with the equitable interest suffers loss as a result of the Registry official's mistake, he must sue the Registry, which owes him a duty of care, in the tort of negligence, and recover financial compensation from the Registry for what he has lost.

Secondly, we have seen that the purchaser will only know what names to include on his search form because he has looked at the title deeds and seen the names of the estate owners through whom the seller traces his title. As we have already seen, a purchaser today is obliged only to go back when investigating title to a fifteen-year minimum period. In the example used in the previous chapter (see page 163), P was not required, and indeed is not entitled, to see the conveyance from A to B thirty years ago. What if, when A acquired the title, he had entered into a restrictive covenant with X, the vendor, and X had registered this covenant against the name of A, the estate owner at the time the covenant was made? P will have no way of discovering this registration, because D is not required to produce the first conveyance from A to B, so that P will have no means of discovering that A ever owned the land he wishes to buy. Because he has no way of discovering this, he will not enter A's name on the search form which he sends off to the Land Charges Registry. At the same time, the covenant has been registered, and, as we have seen, the fact of registration constitutes actual notice to the whole world. Thus P is taken to have actual notice of the covenant, and so to be bound by it, even though, because of the rules about how far back a purchaser is entitled to ask for title to be proved, P had no way of finding out about A's existence. In this situation, P will take subject to X's equitable interest, but if P suffers financial loss as a result, he can seek compensation from the state in respect of that loss. (See Section 25, LPA 1969).

Registered conveyancing

The essence of this scheme is to substitute centralized registration procedures for the bundle of private documents by which title had previously been proved and transferred. At a certain point in time, a transaction involving an old unregistered title would lead to a moment of first registration. Normally, this occurs when the geographical area in which the land is situated is designated an area of compulsory registration. On, for example, the sale of an unregistered title in this area, the purchaser would send all the documents of title which he acquired through the transaction in the old way to the Land Registry, where the title would be given a number, the information contained in the documents transferred to index cards, and the documents cancelled. From that time on, all dealings with the title would be on the basis of the entries in the Registry; the original documents now ceasing to have any effect in law and becoming no more than quaint relics. The title number is crucial to the way the system works. Information storage and retrieval (e.g. for investigation of title) operate with reference to this number.

Once a title has become registered in the way just described, future dealings with it are mediated by the Registry. Investigation of title becomes primarily a matter of ascertaining what information is recorded in the Registry under the title number; and a transfer of title involves forwarding a deed of transfer, drawn up privately between the parties to the transaction, to the Land Registry. The actual transfer of title is effected by the Registry substituting the purchaser's name for that of the vendor as registered proprietor.

Information is recorded on index cards filed under the title number in the Registry under three headings or 'registers' – the 'Property' register which summarises all the rights that go with the title, the 'Charges' register where incumbrances affecting the title are recorded, and the 'Proprietorship' register, where the name of the registered proprietor for the time being is entered along with a statement as to the quality of his title (absolute, good leasehold, qualified or possessory) and any limitations upon his or her freedom to deal with the title. This information is collected together on the 'land certificate', which functions as a summary of the state of the title from time to time, and must be produced for inspection in the majority of transactions and subsequently returned for alteration in the Registry.

'Long' leases (i.e. leases with a significant market value in their own right, and, in particular, all leases with over forty years to run) are given an independent title number. Leases with between twenty-one and forty years to run can be protected in this way if the Registry approves, or by the entry of a 'notice' on the landlord's title, and thus operate as what are called 'minor interests'. This procedure is described below. Leases for under twenty one years are kept off the register and are protected as 'overriding interests'. These too are outlined in due course.

The benefit of easements is normally entered in the property register and thus forms part of the description of the land to which the title relates; the burden, correspondingly, is normally noted in the charges register against the title of the servient landowner. However, as we shall see, if an easement is not registered, it will bind a purchaser of the servient land as an 'overriding interest'.

MINOR INTERESTS

This is a new term introduced by the LRA. It is a general category which embraces a range of mechanisms for protecting interests, claims and rights adverse to or encumbrances on a registered title. It does not refer to some distinctive type of property right (as in 'legal interest' or 'equitable interest').

There are four mechanisms: (1) the restriction; (2) the inhibition; (3) the notice; (4) the caution. To understand the logic of these mechanisms, it is necessary to keep in mind what kind of practical protection a particular type of incumbrance or claim adverse to a title requires if it is to be effectively protected against the owner or prospective purchaser of that title.

Restrictions and inhibitions are entered in the proprietorship register and limit the circumstances in which the Registrar will permit the registered proprietor to deal with the title. For our purposes, the entry of a restriction on the title can be employed to ensure compliance with the 'two-trustee' rule in one of its various forms. For example, a restriction can be used to ensure payment of purchase money to the trustees of the settlement under the SLA, in which case the Registrar will not enter the purchaser as new proprietor unless the restriction has been complied with. Or again, where land is held on a trust for sale (express or statutory) a restriction can be entered requiring any disposition of the title to be made by at least two trustees, thereby indirectly ensuring the protection of the purchaser from the beneficial interests behind the trust (details of which are excluded from the register – see LRA, section 74, and below).

A notice involves the entry of information on the charges register, indicating for example that the title is subject to a restrictive covenant, or that some other adverse interest has been entered against the title. Any prospective purchaser will be alerted to the existence of such claims, which should be protected by a notice on investigating the title. The term 'notice' here is simply LRA-speak, but, obviously, its affinity with the old system and its terminology lies in the fact that it is intended to provide a purchaser with actual notice of incumbrances which may decisively affect his willingness to proceed with respect to the vendor's title.

A caution is just that: a warning, rather than a 'notice', a direct communication, to the enquiring purchaser. Here we are concerned with what is known as the 'caution against dealings' with the registered title. It works as follows. (1) The person with a claim against the title which is capable of protection under LRA 1925, section 54, must make a statutory declaration outlining the nature of his claim. (2) This is sent to the Registry and a caution is entered against the title. (3) This entitles the cautioner to be notified of any proposed dealing with the title. (4) He then has 14 days to enter an objection. (5) Equally the registered proprietor can apply to have the caution removed (as where a prospective purchaser discovers the caution during his inquiries and indicates that he will not continue until the caution is removed); the cautioner will be notified and has fourteen days to make his case. It is primarily for the Land Registrar to decide, in accordance with the LRA and the LR Rules, what course of action is appropriate in such circumstances, though his discretion is ultimately subject to the jurisdiction of the Chancery Division of the High Court.

OVERRIDING INTERESTS
The registered conveyancing scheme was designed to render obsolete the practices of investigation and proof of title associated with the old documentary system. In broad terms – and subject to the general 1925 strategy regarding trusts of land – registration was seen as a functional equivalent of or improvement upon private documents. In this sense, the register was intended to be a 'mirror' of the title. But it was never intended that the register should be comprehensive. Short-term or trivial information, or information which would have been apparent, in accordance with normal pre-1926 conveyancing practice, on inspecting the land, was to be excluded from the register. (There seems to have been a clear desire to prevent the register from becoming over-cluttered in the way that private documentary titles had in the past.)

So the scheme carried over from the old system the practice of inspection of the land, broadly making those rights, often non-documentary in origin, which would previously have been so discoverable, enforceable without entry on the register. In LRA-speak, such rights are called overriding interests.

LRA 1925, section 70, begins –

> All registered land shall, unless under the provisions of this Act the contrary is expressed on the register, be deemed to be subject to such of the following overriding interests as may be for the time being subsisting in reference thereto, and such interests shall not be treated as incumbrances within the meaning of this Act . . .

and then follows a list of items, of varying practical importance, not normally discoverable from the old paper title. These include:

1. Section 70(1)(a):'Rights of common, drainage rights, customary rights . . . public rights, profits *à prendre*, rights of sheepwalk, rights of way, water courses, rights of water and other easements . . .'

Under the new scheme, the benefit of legal easements was expected to be entered in the property register under the title number of the dominant tenement, just as, before 1926, its enforceability would normally depend upon appropriate documentary proof by the person claiming the right. The burden of the easement would not normally have appeared in the servient owner's title deeds.

2. Section 70(1)(b):'Liability to repair highways by reason of tenure, quit-rents, crown-rents, heriots and other rents and charges . . . having their origin in tenure.'

Section 70(1)(j):'Rights of fishing and sporting, seignorial and manorial rights of all descriptions . . . and franchises.'

These kinds of rights were already heading, fairly rapidly, for the dustbin of history; they were included in the scheme 'just in case'.

3. Section 70(1)(f):'subject to the provisions of this Act, rights acquired or in the course of being acquired under the Limitation Acts.'

Obviously, such rights as a squatter possessed would not have appeared in the vendor's paper title, and indeed, as we have seen at page 46 above, many years might elapse before any documentation relating to the squatter's title came into existence. The LRA scheme accommodated itself to these practical realities, providing additionally that a 'successful' squatter (i.e. one who had, through possession of the land adverse to the superior title for the requisite period, barred the assertability of that title's rights vis-à-vis his own) could seek rectification of the register and have his name entered as proprietor instead.

4. Section 70(1)(k):'Leases for any term or interest not exceeding twenty-one years, granted at a rent without taking a fine.'

As we have seen, the landlord-tenant relationship can come into existence in two ways – by a deed under seal or purely verbally, i.e. with or without paper. If the relationship is fixed to last for more than three years, a deed must be used. Informal tenancies were of a shorter duration: commonly from week to week for working-class housing and year to year for agricultural tenancies. Middle-class residential lettings were commonly for two or three years under seal. The intention of this paragraph was to exclude these latter from the register, since in practice the existence of such tenancies would be apparent on inspecting the land, and the extent of the tenant's rights ascertainable from the lease itself.

5. The category of overriding interest which has caused the most difficulty in modern conditions is that set out in section 70(1)(g):'The rights of every person in actual occupation of the land or in receipt of the rents and profits thereof, save where enquiry is made of such person and the rights are not disclosed.'

With what in mind was section 70(1)(g) designed? The answer seems to be connected with the pre-1925 decision in *Hunt v. Luck* (1901),[22] and to be related to the somewhat similar provision contained in LPA 1925, section 14: 'Part I of this Act shall not prejudicially affect the interests of any person in possession or in actual occupation of land to which he may be entitled in right of such possession or occupation.'

In *Hunt v. Luck,* a widow brought an action in the Chancery Division claiming to be entitled to a number of houses in Wimbledon which had belonged to her husband. Two conveyances existed, dating from 1896, two years before his death, by which he apparently transferred these properties to X, who used the conveyances as security for a loan he then raised. These documents of title were, consequently, in the possession of the mortgagees, and it was against them that the widow brought her action; X had since died and his heir did not make an appearance. The widow failed to persuade the court that the conveyances could be set aside as forgeries or because of her husband's incapacity. This left only the argument that there never had been a genuine sale, that the purchase price had never in fact been paid (although one of the conveyances was expressed to be made in consideration of £12,000, and receipt of this sum was expressly acknowledged), and that the mortgagees were fixed with notice of her husband's rights at the time of the mortgage transaction, and of the fact that X, the mortgagor, had no interest in the property.

The houses were occupied by, for the most part, weekly tenants, who paid their rent to a local estate agent. For about two years after the 1896 conveyances, this agent had paid over these rents to the husband. After his death, the agent paid them to X until X also died. (After that, presumably, the agent held on to the collected rents while the dispute was sorted out.) The widow's argument was that the mortgagees, when investigating the title which was to provide security for the loan they were proposing to make, should have asked the tenants who received the rents they paid, and that, on finding this out, they should have gone on to ask – at very least, because he was an estate agent – on whose behalf he was collecting the rents.

The judge concluded that '(1) A tenant's occupation is notice of all that tenant's rights, but not of his lessor's title or rights; (2) actual knowledge that the rents are paid by the tenants to some person whose receipt is inconsistent with the title of the vendor is notice of that person's rights' (1901 1 Ch. at 51). The judge went on: 'Many landlords have agents, and there is nothing inconsistent with the title shewn to the mortgagees . . . in the fact that the rents of the property were collected by a house agent.' The mere fact of payment to an agent could not fix a purchaser with notice. But even if such an extension of the requirements could be envisaged, it could not apply on facts like those of *Hunt v. Luck*, where, thought the judge, '. . . the mortgagees rely on the husband's signature and receipt, and the plaintiff the widow is attempting to fix them with constructive notice of facts which would make it their duty to distrust and disbelieve that signature' (ibid., at 51–2).

The judge's view of the merits frames the central point just as sharply: '. . . even assuming both parties to the action to be equally innocent, the man [i.e. the husband] who has been swindled by too great confidence in his own agent, [i.e. X] has surely less claim to the assistance of a court of equity than a purchaser for value who gets the legal estate, and pays his money without actual notice [i.e. the mortgagees]' (ibid., at 48).

What could indicate more clearly the priorities of practical men in whose environment paper titles could not always be suspect, even if it was too much to hope that, in every case, they be above suspicion?

Section 70(1)(g) seems to have been targeted at the (limited) questions addressed by this case (though as drafted, it is far from clear whether it sought to follow or extend the rule enunciated in that case: was 'in receipt of rent and profits' to be confined to 'notice' of the estate agent or did it extend necessary enquiry to the ultimate recipient of the rents?).

At the core of the issue to which the paragraph is addressed is the question of what observable facts, on inspection of the land, should count as inconsistencies with the title. Before 1925, the title was a paper title; now, it is registered title. But the issue is the same. So what is to count as an inconsistency (as a fact which, once observed, should put the purchaser on enquiry) cannot but be a matter of judicial perception, filtered through sociocultural norms concerning property relations between people. Where a vendor offers a good paper title (or, in LRA terms, is registered as sole proprietor), does the presence of his or her spouse, sibling, lover, child, parent or aged relative suggest anything 'inconsistent' with the title? However, this question is in turn subject to a further question. Does it make a difference that the old flexibility available to judges on conveyancing questions has been constrained, perhaps severely, by the enactment of the 1925 code?

This raises first the problem of how the legislation should be interpreted. We have explored at length in this book those features of landownership in England which explain why contemporary land law is put together in the way it is. But the question is then whether the purposes of the 1925 legislation are relevant to its interpretation today. A long time has passed since its enactment and, as we have seen, many features of the world which its draftsmen took for granted have dissolved. The modern judicial tendency has been to insist that the words of the code should be given their ordinary natural meaning. So, it is now said, with reference to the question of the meaning of section 70(1)(g), that 'rights' means property rights and 'in actual occupation' is a mere question of fact. So if, today, we ask whether the equitable interests arising behind trusts are over-riding interests where the holders of the interests are in occupation of land, and therefore bind purchasers without any requirement that such interests be protected by some form of registration, the answer seems to be that they do, because the interests are 'rights', and *ex hypothesi* they fall within the 'actual occupation' element of the paragraph.

Whether this result is that intended by the draftsmen is another matter. We saw in Chapter 4 that one consequence of the 1925 strategy was to push into equity most of the fragments of title which prior to the code had taken effect at law. We have also indicated that, for the purposes of processing the new types of dispute which have arisen, against the backdrop of the rise of owner-occupation and the informal, 'extra-legal' mode of acquiring the 'rights' which the courts came to recognise, new kinds of 'equities' have come to be formulated by the courts: the new version of implied trust, estoppel and contractual licences. It was suggested above that however diverse the conceptual origins of each of these rights might have been, lawyers of the past would have regarded most of them – with the possible exception of the contractual licence, which is more like a tenancy operative only in equity – as some kind of trust. So if we ask how these new developments should be accommodated within the new arrangements adopted in 1925, it seems sensible to begin by looking more closely at what provision was made for trusts of land when a title to land was being transferred. The scheme of registered conveyancing, precisely because it marked a more radical break with the traditional mechanisms, provides the better starting point for the exploration of this question.

Section 74 of the Land Registration Act 1925 reads as follows: 'Subject to the provisions of this Act as to settled land, neither the registrar nor any person dealing with a registered estate or charge shall be affected with notice of a trust express implied or constructive, and references to trusts shall, so far as possible, be excluded from the register.'

As we have seen, one of the principal extensions of the trust introduced in 1925 to tackle conveyancing difficulties was in the area of settled land, that is, land subjected to strict settlements. It is characteristic of the whole scheme that how settled land was to be accommodated within the new arrangements was dealt with explicitly. Settled land was required to be registered in the name of the tenant for life.

The successive interests created under the settlement were to operate as minor interests. The entry of a restriction in the proprietorship register was envisaged as the way of protecting such interests. The restriction would require production of a receipt for the proceeds of sale from the 'independent' trustees of the settlement before any sale by the tenant for life was recognised, that is, before any purchaser from a tenant for life, making title under the powers conferred upon him by the Settled Land Act, would be entered in the register as the new registered proprietor.

As the Act expresses it: 'There shall also be entered on the register such restrictions as may be prescribed, or may be expedient, for the protection of the rights of the person beneficially interested in the land, and such restrictions shall (subject to the provisions of this Act relating to releases by the trustees of a settlement and to transfers by a tenant for life whose estate has ceased in his lifetime) be binding on the proprietor during his life, but shall not restrain or otherwise affect a disposition by his personal representative.'

Trusts, in other words, were to be kept from the register and were not to affect purchasers. Here, too, the 'best practice' of the old system was carried through into the new. Unsurprisingly, the draftsmen worked upon the old assumptions, and the LRA provisions relating to trusts of land take it for granted that information relating to title should be kept separate from information relating to beneficial interests taking effect behind trusts. The latter, under the new regime, were to be nothing to do with the purchaser, who, it was hoped, need only be concerned with title.

Such was the vision. The difficulty has been: how do the new equities, outlined above, which the courts have been forced to develop, fit in at this point, especially since these equities are, for the most part, intimately connected with the occupation of land, to such an extent, indeed, that in many cases they are best described as equities to occupy?

The question in fact illustrates very well how much of English law works. The judges have now effectively said that these equities will bind purchasers and mortgagees, as overriding interests within section 70(1)(g) in the registered conveyancing system, and, it is assumed, through the doctrine of notice in the increasingly peripheral old system of transfer through title deeds. One court has, indeed, gone further and held that the overriding status of a beneficiary takes precedence over the two-trustee rule.[23] So if granny has a share in equity which affects the title because she put her savings into the construction of an annexe to her son's house for her to live in, her interest will, under this ruling, bind a mortgagee who comes later upon the scene, even though the house is in the joint names of the son and his wife.

One final problem can be noted. Any legal system of adjudication of disputes arising out of land transfer can anticipate disputes which are grounded in the claim that someone has acted badly. What should a court do, for example, if it is faced with a collusive transaction in which title is transferred to a purchaser so as to defeat the rights of someone who has an interest which is not protected by registration when it needs to be, and where both vendor and purchaser know of this fact? Should the purchaser succeed if he pleads that the interest in question is void against him for non-registration under the statute?[24] It is often said that to force the purchaser to take subject to the interest despite the statute because he knew about it is to reintroduce the doctrine of notice which the statute sought to eliminate. Such an argument rather overstates the issue. The LRA, as we have seen, set out to replace paper titles with registered titles, and the information retrievable from them (and thus 'constructive notice') with information retrievable from registers. Merely to say that someone who actually knows of an interest and engages in a transaction clearly designed to take advantage of the statute – especially in a non-commercial context – should be deprived of the benefit of the statute is not to reintroduce all the baggage of constructive notice from the past. Indeed, cases of this sort, in the past, were commonly regarded as instances where it was not possible to formulate general rules, precisely because it turned on the judge's impression of the individual facts of the case whether, in all the circumstances, the purchaser had behaved so badly that the court should intervene.

So pervasive, however, is the theme of 'certainty' in both

academic and judicial legal discourse that it is necessary to direct some general remarks to this question in the concluding chapter which now follows.

9

Conclusion

By contrast with some other areas of property law, the categories of English land law have ceased in large measure to mirror social relations in the way they once did. No doubt one can say that the reason for this is that land, by contrast with other things whose existence seems quite 'natural' in our world, has been around as long as people and therefore as long as human thought. And land has often been thought of as 'different'. In the medieval and early modern period, philosophers and theologians debated the relative merits of land and moveables – especially money – so far as the relationship between virtue or the good life and the ownership of property was concerned. In the eighteenth century, the analysis of wealth and where it came from divided over whether it was land or moveable property which was the fundamental source of wealth. In the nineteenth century, the rather overenthusiastic Henry George could observe that 'The real and natural distinction is between things which are the produce of labour and things which are the gratuitous offerings of nature . . . between wealth and land' (n.d.:239) from which it followed that 'Let the parchments be ever so many, or possession ever so long, natural justice can recognise no right in one man to the possession and enjoyment of land that is not equally the right of all his fellows. Though his titles have been acquiesced in by generation after generation, to the landed estates of the Duke of Westminster the poorest child that is born in London today has as much right as his eldest son' (ibid.:241). At the same period, George Brodrick argued for the abolition of life estates in land though not in personal property. As he put it, 'The policy of prohibiting life-estates in land, without prohibiting the corresponding life-interests in personality, must stand or fall by the peculiar nature, claims, and obligations of Real Property' (1881:345). 'Not a Session', he wrote, 'elapses in which Parliament does not affirm the principle that land

196

is a thing *sui generis*, over which the State may and ought to assume a control far more stringent than it would be politic to assume, but not than it might rightfully assume, over other kinds of property' (ibid.).

What happened in the end, as we have seen, was the preservation of a special legal regime for the transfer of title to land. Quite a lot of the baggage of the past was simply scrapped, and this baggage, for the most part, has been ignored in this book. But elements of the past did remain, and we have tried to give some idea of the antecedents of these elements. Whether what happened in 1925 was radical or not is a matter of perspective. What is barely arguable is the consequence of what happened. Because life estates and entails were not abolished in their entirety but 'relocated' into the realm of equity and lodged by force of statute behind trusts, rather a lot of baggage has survived, albeit in modified form. And so the 1925 legislation, or land law more generally, has become, in many respects, a corpus of learning whose intelligibility and possibly whose very time lies in some respects in the past. In many ways this has been true of land law for many centuries. And it has also long been the case that one of the primary skills of English lawyers lies in adapting the moribund to the needs of the present and land law exemplifies this very well.

But this involves a cost. In a recent working paper, the Law Commission observed that 'it is virtually impossible to draft a mortgage deed that gives a layman any idea of the consequences of entering a mortgage' (1986:4) and that the English law of mortgages 'has never been subjected to systematic statutory reform, and over several centuries of gradual evolution it has acquired a multi-layered structure that is historically fascinating but inappropriately and sometimes unnecessarily complicated' (ibid.:1).

This is true of more than mortgages. In particular, almost every aspect of the law relating to the acquisition, ownership, occupation and transfer of residential property – in other words, of those parts of land law which affect most 'ordinary people' – is 'unnecessarily complicated'. Lawyers, of course, can muddle through as they have always done. Weber was probably right when he wrote, early in this century, that

> The formularies of the conveyancers . . . may be quite unintelligible to the layman, as . . . is the case in England. Yet, he

can understand the basic character of the English way of legal thinking, he can identify with it and, above all, he can make his peace with it by retaining once and for all a solicitor as his legal father-confessor for all contingencies of life, as is indeed done by practically every English businessman (tr. 1978:891).

But it is doubtful that many of today's owner-occupiers and their families retain such confessors. Nor, if the law was more accessible, is there any reason why they should.

It is easy to complain in this vein. It is much more difficult, as we shall repeat, to formulate what should be done. Certainly nothing of that sort can be attempted here. We conclude rather by gathering together the main features of what has been discussed in this book: the nature of English formalism and its connexion with 'history', and the problem of the new informality and its relation to the tradition.

ENGLISH FORMALISM

The energies of conveyancers have always gone into how to get things done. When a conveyancer drafts a will, settlement, lease or restrictive covenant (or rummages through precedent books or standard forms to find something suitable), the ultimate objective is to mediate the intention of this client. Of course, he must tell the client that there are certain things you cannot do, or can do only with great difficulty or risk. But the lawyer's principal task is to find out what the client wants to do, and then to discover the appropriate legal formulae to express in legal language what can usually be said more simply in the language of social or business life.

But if this is to be possible, it requires a relatively stable set of interpretive expectations. If judges keep changing their minds about what all these formulae mean, lawyers will not know where they are, will lack confidence as to the effect of the documents they prepare in the future. This may partly explain why, in times past when the communication network of law was much less systematized than it is now, judges took so seriously, or made such heavy weather of, the task of construction.

One final point about English formalism must be emphasised. It is about stylization. The ideal – which in the nature of things can never be realized – would be to have a formula to meet every wish of every client. Obviously, in the social world, new things are always happening. Old formulae prove insufficient to meet what people want to do. New ones have to be invented, usually by modifying old ones, and the process begins again.

Given this formalist tradition, 'private law' really amounts to engendering a state of affairs in which owners of property can make the law concerning their property within the limits set by the public, general law (as in the perpetuity rules). A lease of a building, for example, gives the law to that building. The parties – usually the lessor – make the rules; the courts, if there is a dispute, are there to provide stable interpretations of that law as expressed in the formulae, and to provide, through their auxiliary agencies, the coercive back-up if need be.

Conveyancers can go on doing things for a long time without anyone other than themselves noticing. The longer they go on doing something, naturally, a professional view as to its nature grows up. Then, for whatever reason, there is a dispute which results in the matter receiving judicial scrutiny. Private litigation costs money and always has. It is relatively rare, in property matters as in others, for people to litigate for the sake of establishing or 'developing' the law. Most private litigation grows out of a conflict of interest in the social world; legal disputation is simply how that conflict is fielded in court and during the run-up to such proceedings in the wranglings between lawyers. A challenge to a lawyers' practice, then, mounted in court, is nearly always just a means, an instrument once again, for the pursuit of the matter at hand.

Unlike most ordinary contracts, many land transactions have effects which stretch over long periods of time. For example, a question can arise in litigation concerning the effect today of a covenant made many years ago. Suppose then that a covenant is made, say, one hundred years ago, and the appropriate formula of the time is used to annex the benefit so it will run with the land in the future. Years later, part of the land is sold off. Then the question arises in court: after the sale, does the seller or the buyer have the right to enforce the covenant? How should we assess whatever decision is arrived at by a judge?

1. How can we tell if the judge is right or wrong? If the question has come up for decision before, and the judge has followed that

199

decision, we would usually say he has done what he should. The older that decision was, the more justified the judge is today in following it, for reasons we will shortly see.

2. If our judge's decision is new, that is, the question has been decided for the first time, how then do we evaluate it? First, we can ask whether it is in accordance with conveyancing opinion. Even assuming that contemporary opinion on the point is unanimous – which it sometimes is not – there is still a further question. Is it contemporary opinion which is relevant, or conveyancing opinion at the time the covenant was made? The latter is of course really an historical question, and neither judges nor conveyancers are primarily historians. In the end it must be contemporary opinion which will prevail, even if such opinion, on points like this, might lay emphasis on whatever happens to be the received wisdom among today's conveyancers about the practices of the past, rather than a serious answer to a serious historian's question. If the judge has followed this opinion in giving his decision, all is well. Indeed, he ought to find reasons if he wishes to depart from this opinion. The question, after all, as so often, is pre-eminently a conveyancer's question: what is the effect of a particular verbal formula?

3. What 'policy' reasons might a judge put forward for departing from conveyancing opinion on this kind of question? Today, of course, people argue about whether restrictive covenants, as the principal form of private land use control, should continue to operate in an era of public law planning regulation. But it is hardly open to a judge to adopt such a reason for his decision, when people have conducted their affairs on the basis that such covenants will be effective and when such covenants have received judicial recognition for so long. And very few judges indeed would see it as their role to decide a case on such a basis. There is however another policy reason which is not always spelt out. We could call it 'in-house' policy. Maybe because it is in-house, it is often overlooked by law students and legal commentators alike. This is where a judge feels that his – or more generally, judicial – time is being wasted on 'empty questions'. In such circumstances, a judge may be tempted to decide a case so as to stop litigation in the future on similar questions. However, on points where conveyancing opinion is relatively settled, a judge who flies in the face of it is likely to generate rather than stem the flood of litigation.

4. A judge who has gone against conveyancing opinion without the support of existing judicial authority can fairly be said to have changed the rules. Now no one knows how many covenants there are. The only 'control' over them, apart from judicial willingness or unwillingness to enforce them, is at the point of their production: in particular, conveyancers' know-how. So if our judge has gone against prevailing opinion, he has changed the rules retrospectively. It is possible, though no one knows, because we work in conditions of high uncertainty, (which is why conveyancing opinion is so important), that 'out there' are thousands of covenants whose writers used the particular annexation formula, whose legal effect our hypothetical judge has now changed. All of these covenants, contrary to expectation, would now be unenforceable as a result of the decision of the judge. Most people would probably say, intuitively, that there is something not right about that.

5. However, in terms of the future, the judge's decision has a largely technical effect. A new formula will be created by conveyancers for the standard forms, precedent books and advice manuals. This will only happen, of course, if conveyancers find out about the decision. One can hardly overemphasise the importance for grasping the degree of systematisation of the legal system of thinking of it as a communication network.

ANTI-HISTORICISM AND THE IMPRINT OF THE PAST

These tensions are not confined to the construction of formulae contained in private documents. They arise equally with the interpretation of land law statutes, and for very similar reasons. First, the statutes too abound with formulaic expressions; they are written in the language of conveyancers of long ago. Secondly, as has been stressed, the principal statutes themselves are now over sixty years old. And so, with statutes as with conveyancing practice, the question is posed of what is the nature of an English lawyer's attitude towards the past. Is English adjudication an historical enquiry? The answer is that sometimes it is and sometimes it is not. But 'history' is just a method, a technique, which along with others enables counsel to formulate arguments and a judge to provide reasons for why he has resolved a dispute in the way he has. There is no normative hierarchy regulating judicial method. It is unsystematic, a matter of 'appropriateness', of practical experience. This has several consequences for the student of land law. First, since the shapes of the past are so deeply imprinted upon the fabric of the modern law of property, these shapes can be made more accessible by studying some of the practices of the past. But, secondly, since judicial resort to 'history' is, so to speak, opportunistic, the reader of contemporary judicial decisions will find that past ignored as often as it is considered. Thirdly, the student encounters, in textbooks and in judgements, the assertion of long continuities, the removal of a judicial dictum from its (time-bound, historical) context and its insertion into a timeless plain of 'fundamental principle'. That is, the more sensitive to historical context the student of the subject becomes, the more he or she is likely to encounter a peculiar kind of history in the pages of the law.

NONFORMALISM

Where there is formalism, we are likely to encounter its opposite, at least in an environment in which, as is the case in England, people have better things to do than spend their time in the offices of, or on the telephone to, their lawyers, if they have one at all. Yet the English approach to land law and to trusts largely presupposed a familiarity, in every sense of the word, with your lawyer, who was literally your *chargé d'affaires*.

Where people arrange their affairs without the assistance of lawyers, it is obviously the case that lawyers will get involved in trying to make legal sense of the relationship only in the event of a dispute of some kind. But there is nothing new about the need to make sense of informal arrangements, about the need for the interpretation of facts rather than documents, in the adjudicative process. The tenancy at will, outlined in Chapter 5, provides one example, and disputes over the liability to pay rates or over the eligibility to vote, when the franchise was restricted by a property qualification, provide other examples of when courts were called upon to determine the 'true legal nature' of an informal arrangement which lawyers had not been able – and would not have expected to have been called upon – to pin down in advance by formalising it.

These were not the kinds of matters which taxed the draftsmen of the 1925 code to any great extent, because, more or less by definition, they were marginal to the principal concerns of conveyancers. Their 'conveyancing implications' were peripheral to what was at issue in 1925, since they amounted to little more than the familiar, routine matter of finding a place in the new schemes for the old practices of inspection of the land, outlined in Chapter 7. The development of the new residential 'equities', precipitated by the rise of owner-occupation, which we sketched in Chapter 4 and whose conveyancing implications were outlined in Chapter 8, has thrown up what seems, in one sense, to be a quite new set of problems. They threaten to disrupt the unconscious design of English property law, because most of these equities[25] – even the contractual licence as it has come to be formulated in the residential context – import some notion of trust. And trust brings us back to the domain of English formalism.

Informality and its consequences, so far as trusts were concerned, arose against the backdrop of the formalism already considered. The normative expectations appropriate to that formalist and formulaic tradition could be brought into play in the adjudication of disputes. This was true in two obvious respects. First, long practice could itself generate normative expectations. The contents of formal instruments prepared by lawyers in relation to property not only became standardised as part and parcel of the formulaic tradition, but 'typified' or 'paradigmatic'. Judges who had been conveyancers would in the nature of things have a set of ideas about how people of property ought to arrange their affairs, and even those who had not practised as conveyancers would have received similar advice in the management of their own personal affairs, and this 'good sense' would be reinforced by counsel in the courtroom.

Secondly, formalism and the expectations generated by it serve as a backdrop for adjudication in the sense that lawyers and judges come to typify the circumstances in which they expect people to organise their affairs with their assistance, through their instrumentality. The more reasonable it seems to lawyers to expect that people will invoke their assistance to arrange their affairs in a formal way, especially concerning the disposition of their property, the more justifiable it seems to impose strict limits on the circumstances in which the courts will afford assistance to those whose claims are without a formal basis.[26]

What then is not new is judges drawing upon non-legal normative resources – however these are generated – in the course of resolving disputes between parties whose relations, from a legal point of view, are informal. What is new today is not directly attributable to the judiciary, but to the wider social world with whose conflicts they have to deal from time to time, in which the formalism of lawyers has in large measure disappeared.

This is the range of social relationships which arise informally against the backdrop of owner-occupation. Because these relationships concern property, and do not just appear on its margins, lawyers are supposed to have answers to basic questions to do with people's rights in such situations. The reason why it is difficult to give clear answers when these are sought in the event of a dispute is not least because not even any backdrop of formal legal practice exists to provide a 'typified' point of reference, just diffuse sets of social norms which may in any event, in a modern society, be very divergent.

For some, the solution lies in more legislation: to codify in some way rights of occupation. How far this would help is not clear. But most difficult of all is to work out what criteria should stand as a measure for whatever is proposed. It is not very difficult to work out some conveyancing regime which is less abstruse than the one which we use today. What is difficult is to decide, and to decide how to decide, where to place the priorities, how to allocate the risks. Secondly, if the case law on the acquisition of occupation or ownership rights in respect of owner-occupied property is a mess, from what standpoint can anyone propose something better? It is one thing to recognise the nature of judicial activity, that is, to demystify some of the pomposities in which it is encased; it is another to suggest that a more satisfactory way of proceeding can be achieved, in general terms, through statutory law reform, because such a project begs the question of whose values are to determine the necessarily generalised shape of anything which might be proposed.

Notes

1. A notable exception is Lawson and Rudden, 1982.
2. For the Justinian codification, see Honoré, 1978; for the influence of the Roman textbook, the Institutes, see Kelley, 1979; for the ways in which modern civilian systems departed from the Roman example, see Jolowicz, 1957; on codification and property, see Strakosch, 1967.
3. See *South Staffordshire Water Co. v. Sharman* [1896] 2 QB 44; *City of London Corporation v. Appleyard* [1965] 1 WLR 000; *Parker v. British Airways Board* [1982] 1 All ER 834.
4. *Asher v. Whitlock* (1865) LR 1 QB 1.
5. Critchley, 1978, usefully summarises the general issues; for the problems of 'feudalism' as an analytical tool for the understanding of the Middle Ages, see Brown, 1973.
6. See Bean, 1968 and cf. Milsom, 1981.
7. Earl of Oxford's Case (1616).
8. *Duke of Somerset v. Cookson* 3 PW 390.
9. Lord Loughborough C., *Fells v. Read* 3 V 71.
10. *Maddison v. Alderson* (1883) 8 App Cas 467.
11. *Lace v. Chantler* [1944] KB 368.
12. For what follows, see especially Horn, 1980; Beckett, 1986.
13. For what follows, see Dennis, 1984; Daunton, 1983; and note Swenarton and Taylor, 1985.
14. *Expert Clothing v. Hillgate House* [1985] 3 WLR 359.
15. *National Carriers Ltd v. Panalpina (Northern) Ltd* [1981] 2 WLR 45.
16. Some recent exceptions, or judgments which present themselves as exceptions, are *Street v. Mountford* [1985] 2 WLR 877; *NWB v. Morgan* [1985] 1 All ER 821.
17. Leasehold Reform Act 1967.
18. See *Walsh v. Lonsdale* (1882) 21 Ch D 9; *Manchester Brewery v. Coombs* [1901] 2 Ch. 608.
19. Another means, of uncertain scope, is suggested in the judgments in *Halsall v. Brizell* (1957) Ch 169 and *E.R. Ives Investment Ltd v. High* (1967) 2 QB 379.

20. 12 Ch D 31.
21. There seem to be two exceptions to this: a bare trust and the constructive trust as formulated in *Binions v. Evans* [1972] Ch 359.
22. 1 Ch. The quotations here and on the following pages are at 45, 57, 51–2 and 48 respectively.
23. *City of London Properties v. Flegg* [1986] 2 WLR 616. The case is now on appeal.
24. cf. *Peffer v. Rigg* [1977] 1 WLR 285 and *Midland Bank Trust Co v. Green* [1981] AC 513.
25. For an exception, see Murphy and Clark, 1983:120–123.
26. *Maddison v. Alderson*, *supra*, can be viewed in this light.

Bibliography

Anderson, J. Stuart (1984), 'Land Law Texts and the Explanation of 1925', *Current Legal Problems*.

Atiyah, P.S. (1978), 'Contracts, Promises and the Law of Obligations', *Law Quarterly Review*.

Bean, J.M.W. (1968), *The Decline of English Feudalism*, Manchester: University of Manchester Press.

Beckett, J.V. (1986), *The Aristocracy in England 1660–1914* Oxford: Basil Blackwell.

Bourdieu, Pierre (1972, tr. 1977 by Richard Nice), *Outline of a Theory of Practice*, Cambridge: Cambridge University Press.

Brodrick, George C. (1881), *English Land and English Landlords*, London: Cassel, Petter, Galpin.

Brown, E.A.R. (1973), 'The Tyranny of a Construct: Feudalism and Historians of Medieval Europe', *American Historical Review*.

Bullen, Edward (1899), second edition by Cyril Dodd and T.J. Bullen, *The Law of Distress*, London: Butterworth.

Cannadine, David (1977), 'Aristocratic Indebtedness in the Nineteenth Century: The Case Re-Opened', *Economic History Review, 2nd ser.*

Clanchy, M.T. (1979), *From Memory to Written Record*, London: Edward Arnold.

Clark, J.C.D. (1985), *English Society 1688–1832*, Cambridge: Cambridge University Press.

Clark, J.C.D. (1986), *Revolution and Rebellion*, Cambridge: Cambridge University Press.

Clay, Christopher (1968), 'Marriage, Inheritance and the Rise of Large Estates in England, 1660–1815', *Economic History Review, 2nd ser.*

Critchley, John (1978), *Feudalism*, London: George Allen and Unwin.

Daunton, M.J. (1983), *House and Home in the Victorian City,* London: Edward Arnold.

Dennis, Richard (1984), *English Industrial Cities of the Nineteenth Century*, Cambridge: Cambridge University Press.

Edinburgh Review (1821) [C.H. Bellenden Ker].

Ekelund, Robert B. and Tollison, Robert D. (1981), *Mercantilism as a Rent-Seeking Society*, College Station: Texas A and M University Press.

Evans, Eric J. (1976), *The Contentious Tithe*, London: Routledge and Kegan Paul.

George, Henry (n.d.), *Progress and Poverty*, London: J.M. Dent.

Goody, Jack (1983), *The Development of the Family and Marriage in Europe*, Cambridge: Cambridge University Press.

Gudeman, Stephen (1986), *Economics As Culture*, London: Routledge and Kegan Paul.

Hewitt, E.P. and Richardson, J.B. (1928), *White and Tudor's Leading Cases in Equity*, vol. 2, ninth edition, London: Sweet and Maxwell.

Honoré, Tony (1978), *Tribonian*, London: Duckworth.

Hopkins, Keith (1983), *Death and Renewal*, Cambridge: Cambridge University Press.

Horn, Pamela (1980), *The Rural World 1780–1850*, London: Hutchinson.

Jolowicz, H.F. (1957), *Roman Foundations of Modern Law*, Oxford: Clarendon Press.

Kant, Immanuel (1797, tr. 1965 by John Ladd), *The Metaphysical Elements of Justice*, Indianapolis: Bobbs-Merrill.

Kelley, Donald R. (1979), 'Gaius Noster: Substructures of Western Social Thought', *American Historical Review*.

Law Commission (1986), *Land Mortgages (Working Paper No. 99)*, London: HMSO.

Lawson, F.H. and Rudden, B. (1982), *The Law of Property*, second edition, Oxford: Clarendon Press.

Macfarlane, Alan (1978), *The Origins of English Individualism*, Oxford: Basil Blackwell.

Maitland, F.W. (1909), *Equity and the Forms of Action*, Cambridge: Cambridge University Press.

Marx, Karl (1844, tr. 1975 by Clemens Dutt), 'On the Jewish Question', in Karl Marx and Frederick Engels, *Collected Works*, vol. 3, London: Lawrence and Wishart; Moscow: Progress Publishers.

Mauss, Marcel (1925, tr. 1966, 1969 by Ian Cunnison), *The Gift*, London: Routledge and Kegan Paul.

Milsom, S.F.C. (1981), *Historical Foundations of the Common Law*, second edition, London: Butterworths.

Murphy, W.T. and Clark, Hilary (1983), *The Family Home*, London: Sweet and Maxwell.

Musgrove, Frank and Middleton, Roger (1981), 'Rites of Passage and the Meaning of Age in Contrasted Social Groups', *British Journal of Sociology*.

Northrup, David (1978), *Trade Without Rulers*, Oxford: Oxford University Press.

Bibliography

Oakley, Francis (1984), *Omnipotence, Covenant and Order*, London: Cornell University Press.

Offer, Avner (1977), 'Origins of the Law of Property Acts 1910–1925', *Modern Law Review*.

Ryan, Alan (1984), *Property and Political Theory*, Oxford: Basil Blackwell.

Simpson, A.W.B. (1961), *An Introduction to the History of the Land Law*, Oxford: Oxford University Press.

Snell, Edmund H.T. (1908), fifteenth edition by Archibald Brown, *The Principles of Equity*, London: Stevens and Haynes.

Strakosch, Henry E. (1967), *State Absolutism and the Rule of Law*, Sydney: Sydney University Press.

Sugden, E.B. (1858), *A Handy Book on Property Law*, fifth edition, Edinburgh.

Swenarton, Mark and Taylor, Sandra (1985), 'The Scale and Nature of the Growth of Owner-Occupation in Britain between the Wars', *Economic History Review, 2nd ser.*

Thompson, F.M.L. (1955), 'The End of a Great Estate', *Economic History Review*, 2nd ser.

Twiss, Horace (1846), *The Public and Private Life of Lord Chancellor Eldon*, 2 vols, third edition, London: John Murray.

Weber, Max (tr. 1978 by Ephraim Fischoff *et al.*), ed. Guenther Roth and Claus Wittich, *Economy and Society*, Berkeley: University of California Press.

Williams, T. Cyprian (1922), *Vendor and Purchaser*, 2 vols., third edition by T. Cyprian Williams and John M. Lightwood, London: Sweet and Maxwell.

Woodburn, J.C. (1972), 'Ecology, Nomadic Movement and the Composition of the Local Group among Hunters and Gatherers: an East African Example and Its Implications', in Peter J. Ucko *et al.*, eds., *Man, Settlement and Urbanism*, London: Duckworth.

Yelling, J.A. (1977), *Common Field and Enclosure in England 1450–1850*, London: Macmillan.

Index

Index

Index

UNDERSTANDING EQUITY AND TRUSTS

Jeffrey Hackney

Understanding Equity and Trusts seeks to reveal the arguments and reasons underlying this particular aspect of the law, and to encourage the reader to participate in evaluating them.

The Equity jurisdiction, which takes its name from the first principle of justice, began as discretionary intervention, supporting, supplementing and correcting the more ancient common law. It has become a separate system, with its own doctrines and remedies, and dominated by its most substantial and characteristic contribution to the legal system of which it is a part, the trust, which is first and foremost a property-management device of great sophistication, versatility and beauty. This creature has been successfully transformed from its ancient feudal origins to a flourishing commercial mechanism which is a mainstay of every contemporary pension fund manager and tax planner.

Jeffrey Hackney exposes the essential shape and nature of the trust, looking at its social uses and at the wide variety of arrangements and conclusions which pass under its name. His approach is thematic, describing the patterns and the doctrines which underpin the detailed decisions. This is a critical book, assessing from a standpoint of warm admiration the common law's most glorious failure. Written with the minimum of citation, his book transforms an area of law often regarded as arid into one full of life.

UNDERSTANDING
TORT LAW

Carol Harlow

Tort law is the technical name for part of our system of civil liability. When people turn to the legal system for compensation for some injury which they have suffered, the rules of tort law come into play. So tort law has to deal with a wide range of situations. If a careless driver causes an accident, for example, he may be legally liable and he (or more often his insurers) will have to compensate those who have been injured. In a very different case, a householder whose neighbours disturb him by their noise or other annoying habits may want the nuisance ended. He, too, can turn to tort law. So could someone whose reputation has been damaged by a defamatory article in a newspaper. To deal with these disparate situations, tort law needs to be versatile and to keep in tune with changing social needs.

Understanding Tort Law sets out to place the modern rules of tort into their social context in order to help those who are new to the subject to follow its development. It outlines the way in which the rules are made and describes their origins in a very different society. The book also provides a simple introduction to tort law's complex and confusing rules and technical vocabulary.

UNDERSTANDING
CRIMINAL LAW

C. M. V. Clarkson

The main focus of *Understanding Criminal Law* is on the general principles of criminal liability and the most important offences – homicide and the other crimes against the person, sexual offences, and the various property offences such as theft and burglary. It explains the substantive rules of criminal law within the context of the law's overall objectives, showing that the distinction between murder and manslaughter, for instance, can be properly understood only if the law's purpose is also appreciated. In doing this, the rationale of the various rules and the relationship between them is explored. This examination reveals that the criminal law is concerned with protecting certain values. The author exposes these values and subjects them to scrutiny, at times expressing preferences as to how the criminal law should develop. His book presents a straightforward and stimulating approach to understanding criminal law.

UNDERSTANDING PUBLIC LAW

Gabriele Ganz

The British constitution used to be the envy of the world; now there is hardly any element of it which has not come under attack. In exploring why this has happened, *Understanding Public Law* explains how the constitution works today.

The sovereignty of Parliament, once the hallmark of British democracy, has given rise to an elective dictatorship, the government dominating the House of Commons through the party machine. The Prime Minister's power has been growing vis-à-vis the Cabinet and Civil Service. The government increasingly uses delegated legislation, and it has greatly centralized power by imposing constraints on local government and the nationalized industries. There has been no corresponding growth in the mechanisms for accountability or public participation in decision-making. But there has been a considerable extension of police powers of arrest and detention, searching of premises and dealing with public disorder. Fundamental changes to the constitution have been recommended to remedy these defects, such as electoral reform, devolution, a Freedom of Information Act and a Bill of Rights. Without such changes the working of the constitution could be transformed if those elected to power behaved differently. A democracy is only as good as its elected representatives.

Professor Ganz's readable account of the state of public law will both clarify and provoke discussion.

UNDERSTANDING CONTRACT LAW

John Adams and Roger Brownsword

The major contention of *Understanding Contract Law* is that the legal rules regulating agreements cannot be understood without examining what lies behind those rules.

The book seeks to interpret judicial decision-making in contract cases. It portrays judges as caught in a web of tensions. They are pulled in one direction by a wish to keep faith with tradition; and in another direction by a wish to ensure acceptable outcomes to disputes, to meet commercial expectations, and to protect consumers. The outcome of any particular case will depend therefore not on the mechancial application of 'the law of contract' but on the way in which the ideological tensions which structure judges' reasoning are resolved.

This accessible yet challenging analysis of contract law provides a full introduction to the subject and puts forward new ideas.